# Marcher Railways

## The railways of Wrexham and Oswestry, a photographic history

A. Bodlander, M. Hambly,
H. Leadbetter, D. Southern
& S. Weatherley

*Marcher Railways - the railways of Wrexham and Oswestry, a
photographic history*
First published in Wales in 2008
by
**BRIDGE BOOKS**
61 Park Avenue
Wrexham
LL12 7AW

Much of this work was previously published as
*Wrexham Railways, a collection of pictures* (Vols 1 & 2)
and *Oswestry Railways, a collection of pictures*

© 2008  Photographs, maps and text, A. Bodlander, M. Hambly,
H. Leadbetter, D. Southern and S. Weatherley
© 2008 Design, typesetting and layout, Bridge Books

ISBN 978-1-84494-050-9

A CIP entry for this book is available from the British Library

Printed and bound by
Cromwell Press Ltd
Trowbridge

# Contents

**FRONTISPIECE**

The Wrexham, Mold & Connah's Quay and Cambrian Railways station staff at Wrexham Central Station, c.1900, pose alongside Cambrain Railways 0-4-4T, Nº. 3, which has arrived from Ellesmere hauling a rake of six-wheel passenger coaches. [*A. Cliff*]

# Introduction

In many ways, the railways of the Wrexham and Oswestry areas represent a microcosm of the development and subsequent history of the railway network throughout Britain. There were many competing proposals for railways in and through the areas from the 1840s onwards, and the lines ultimately built included both locally-promoted ventures and grander schemes that were primarily passing through. Both towns were also at one time, home to a railway company headquarters and associated workshops; the Cambrian Railways at Oswestry and the Wrexham, Mold & Connah's Quay at Wrexham. Across the area, there were instances of both intense competition and shared working arrangements, and of traffic levels ranging from rural halts providing only a handful of passengers each week, to industrial customers generating sufficient tonnage to keep yards and signal boxes open around the clock. Although not as closely associated with narrow-gauge railways as points further west into north and mid Wales, the area nevertheless included examples of 1' 8", 1' 9$\frac{1}{2}$", 1' 11$\frac{1}{2}$", 2' 0", 2'4$\frac{1}{4}$", 2' 6" and 4' 0" gauge lines in addition to the standard gauge main lines and branches.

The contents table lists in full the lines covered, but in summary the compilers have sought to include the Cambrian main line between Whitchurch and Welshpool, the Tanat Valley and Llanfyllin branches, the Wrexham and Ellesmere Railway, the Great Western's Shrewsbury to Chester main line between Whittington and Rossett, the Wrexham, Mold & Connah's Quay Railway and the network of branches in the Brymbo, Rhos and Ruabon areas.

The photographs selected are intended as far as possible to show the everyday reality of the working railway rather than special events, and to illustrate the work of railwaymen as well as the railway infrastructure and the trains running upon or along it. Although many of the subjects captured have now disappeared into history, there is also a selection of more recent views to bring the story up-to-date, including coverage of some of the railway preservation activities in the area.

Since the publication of the original constituent parts of this book in the early 1990s, there have inevitably been a number of changes. From an organisational perspective, the most significant was undoubtedly the dismantling and privatisation of British Rail, following the passing of the 1993 Railways Act. There has also been increased political interest in, and associated funding for, the rail network and services throughout Wales since the establishment of the National Assembly in 1998.

After a period in which the area's passenger services were provided by a combination of operators, a reorganisation of franchise boundaries brought consolidation under the responsibility of a single operator, Arriva Trains Wales, in 2003. Freight also remains important, with three rail-served industrial locations receiving regular traffic – Corus (formerly British Steel) at Shotton, Castle Cement at Padeswood and Kronospan at Chirk. English, Welsh & Scottish Railway (EWS), now owned by the German railway operator Deutsche Bahn, had a monopoly on freight operations in the area until early in 2007 when Amec Spie began operating timber trains to Chirk from Carlisle. In terms of infrastructure, there have been both losses and gains, with the lifting of the mothballed Brymbo and Gatewen branches and removal of the goods loops at Weston Rhyn, while Wrexham Central station has been rebuilt as part of a new shopping centre and a new passenger train servicing depot has been provided at Wrexham General.

It is fitting that, as this book was being finalised at the end of April 2008, a new open-access train operator, Wrexham and Shropshire Railways, began direct services of up to five trains per day each way between Wrexham and London Marylebone, with most services also calling at Gobowen, the gateway station for Oswestry. Additionally, as part of an enhanced service to Chester and the north Wales coast planned for December 2008, Virgin Trains announced that they would also offer a daily business train from Wrexham General to London Euston and return, running via Chester. If all goes to plan, by the end of 2008 Wrexham General will be the Welsh representative in a very select group of British stations which can boast a choice of long-distance services to London leaving in opposite directions, provided by different operators and serving different London termini.

Adrian Bodlander
Mark Hambly
Harry Leadbetter
Dave Southern
Steve Weatherley

August 2008

# Acknowledgements

Compiling a book such as this is only possible as a result of the generous co-operation of a large number of individuals. Contributing photographers are credited adjacent to their work, but where it has not been possible to trace the source, this is indicated by attribution to the Authors' Collection. Many of the photographs collected came with fascinating memories of the subject depicted or other associated historical detail which in turn informed the text and captions. The staff of record offices, libraries and newspapers at Hawarden, Ruthin, Shrewsbury and Wrexham pointed us towards certain gems in their collections and arranged for the necessary copies to be made. Members of railway staff from the area, past and present, have taken the time to describe routine and unusual working arrangements, colourful characters and the many other aspects of railway practice which go unseen by the uninitiated traveller. Those responsible for the operation of the internal rail systems within the production processes at a number of industrial locations in the area, several of which have now closed, were extremely tolerant of our visits to their plants. Fellow enthusiasts have also been willing to share information, proving many times over that the casual personal notes of yesterday are the valuable archive materials of tomorrow. At the risk of omitting some by naming others, we would particularly like to record the contributions of Revd Alan Cliff, Peter Fisher, John Hobbs and Ivor Owen, as well as the late Frank Jones and Mike Lloyd. Finally we would like to thank Alister Williams of Bridge Books for suggesting that our three original books were worthy of bringing together and developing further into the present volume. Any errors and omissions remain ours, but we would appreciate being informed of them, or of any additional information relating to the subjects depicted, via the publisher.

# The Shrewsbury
# & Chester Railway

By the late 1830s, the slow and circuitous canal route between the industrial areas around Ruabon and the towns of north-west England was regarded as a hindrance to trade, leading in 1839 to the first proposal for a railway from Chester to Wrexham, based on a survey by George Stephenson. This scheme was not pursued because of the economic depression of the early 1840s, but in 1844, a similar scheme was mooted by local colliery and iron works proprietors, principally Henry Robertson and Robert Roy. Their proposal was initially for a railway from Chester to Wrexham but this was later extended to Ruabon. The scheme, under the title of the North Wales Mineral Railway, obtained an Act of Parliament on 6 August 1844 and construction commenced.

At that time, the London & Birmingham Railway was in dispute with the Grand Junction Railway and so the L&B, seeing a possible alternative route to the Mersey avoiding the GJR, supported the projected Shrewsbury and Birmingham Railway and also promoted an extension of the NWMR to join it at Shrewsbury – the Shrewsbury, Oswestry & Cheshire Junction Railway. On 28 August 1846, the SO&CJR amalgamated with the NWMR to form the Shrewsbury & Chester Railway. The first section of the railway opened on 4 November 1846 from Saltney Junction, just outside Chester on the Chester & Holyhead Railway, to Ruabon. There were intermediate stations at Saltney, Pulford & Dodleston, Rossett, Gresford and Wrexham. There was a short branch to a wharf on the Dee at Saltney. A further branch was opened in July 1847 from Wheatsheaf Junction, north of Wrexham, to the industrial centre of Brymbo and on to Minera.

The extension of the line to Shrewsbury was opened to the public on 14 October 1848 with intermediate stations at Cefn, Llangollen Road, Chirk, Preesgweene, Gobowen, Whittington, Rednal, Baschurch and Leaton. Two days prior to the start of public services, a special train of no less than three locomotives and fifty-nine carriages left Chester carrying dignitaries to the inaugural banquet at Shrewsbury. The final branch of the S&C was that from Gobowen to Oswestry which opened on 23 December 1848.

After a peaceful first year, the S&C became seriously involved in Victorian railway politics. In 1846, the L&B amalgamated with the GJR to form the London & North Western Railway which was opposed to the alternative route from the Midlands to the Mersey offered by the S&C and S&B following the opening of the latter in 1849. When the S&C and S&B rashly decided to cut their rates between Wolverhampton and Chester, a

Wrexham's Railways c.1925

clash with the LNWR became inevitable. After five years of pressure tactics, the S&C and S&B sought help from the Great Western Railway who were completing their line from Oxford to Birmingham. As a consequence, the GWR proposed a Bill for amalgamation with the S&C and S&B and conversion of their lines to Brunel's Broad Gauge. The Bill was contested by the LNWR but nevertheless was passed by Parliament, with the exception of the gauge conversion, and so from 1 September 1854, the S&C and S&B became part of the GWR.

Following the arrival of the GWR, stations and services were improved. Johnstown & Hafod station was opened in 1896 followed by Balderton in 1901. During the twentieth century, halts were opened at Rhosrobin, Wynnville, Rhosymedre, Whitehurst (the former Llangollen Road which had been closed following the opening of the Vale of Llangollen Railway), Trehowell, Haughton, Stanwardine and Old Woods. The line also served many of the collieries of the North Wales coalfield, from Gresford in the north to Ifton, over the border in Shropshire, in the south. At its peak, the line had twenty-two stations and halts. Today, only Wrexham, Ruabon, Chirk and Gobowen survive and only Wrexham and Gobowen retain any staff.

# Wrexham General Station

**1. WREXHAM STATION, *c*.1866**
The first Wrexham railway station was constructed by the Shrewsbury and Chester Railway and was in a splendid Jacobean style with distinctive Dutch gable pediments. The architect for the whole of the line was Thomas Penson of Wrexham, who gained particular acclaim for his designs of Shrewsbury and Gobowen stations. In this view the stationmaster, his family and staff pose for the camera. *[A. N. Palmer Centre, Wrexham]*

**2. WREXHAM GENERAL STATION, *c*.1880**
Illustrating how the station was built beyond the western limit of the built-up area along Mold Road, here the roofline of the original station behind the hedge of Crispin Lane. The boundary between the railway and this lane follows the line of the early medieval earthwork Wat's Dyke. *[W. Alister Williams Collection]*

**3. WREXHAM GENERAL STATION, 1905**
The staff of Wrexham General in 1905. Whilst the authority of the stationmaster is evident by the braid on his hat and the lady from the refreshment room is the sole female present, it would be interesting to identify the other staff and the grades at which they served. *[Trefor Thompson Collection]*

**4. WREXHAM GENERAL STATION, *c*.1912**

Following the takeover of the Shrewsbury & Chester line by the Great Western Railway, and the expansion of rail traffic at Wrexham, the facilities of the original building clearly proved to be inadequate and between 1910 and 1912 it was rebuilt to a standardised GWR design. This was in the 'French Pavilion' style, which incorporated decorative iron railings to the roof turrets. Whilst most other stations of this design were built entirely of red brick, the new Wrexham General incorporated stonework and it is interesting to contemplate whether stone from the original building was utilised. The horse bus seen outside the station was owned by the Wynnstay Arms Hotel and served to convey guests to and from the station. [*A. N. Palmer Centre, Wrexham*]

**5. WREXHAM GENERAL, 1917**
The First World War saw the railways of Britain engaged in transporting all manner of military traffic. This photograph, although damaged, shows trench mortar bombs (manufactured by Powell Brothers at their Cambrian Works alongside the station yard) being loaded into a railway van at Wrexham General. The atmosphere of a typical railway yard is captured by the horse on the loading dock with its GWR blanket and the jib of a hand crane visible to the right behind the end of the van.
*[Bersham Industrial Heritage Centre]*

**6. WREXHAM GENERAL, *c.*1950**
GWR 'ROD' Class 2-8-0 3038 passing Wrexham North with a southbound freight. This class of locomotive was originally introduced by the Great Central Railway in 1911 and was adopted by the Railway Operating Department (hence 'ROD') of the Royal Engineers for service in Europe during the First World War. After the war a batch were bought by the GWR who attempted to 'Swindonise' them by fitting their standard safety valve covers and chimneys. *[C. E. Stephens]*

**7. WREXHAM, *c*.1950**

An operating crisis at Wrexham General. The passenger train on the right, hauled by GWR 'Hall' Class 4-6-0 *Adderley Hall,* failed in the section south of Wrexham and was rescued by an unidentified GWR 0-6-0PT. The disgraced 'Hall' is being removed ready for the GWR 2-6-0 on the left to be commandeered from its freight train to take the passenger train forward to Chester. The wooden posted signals make a fine display. Note particularly the smoke deflector on the bracket signal. *[C. E. Stephens]*

*Facing, top:*
**8. WREXHAM, *c*.1950**

GWR 'Manor' Class 4-6-0 7828 *Odney Manor* stands alongside the Goods Depot in early British Railways days with an empty stock train. This locomotive is now preserved and has recently been operating on the West Somerset Railway.
*[C. E. Stephens]*

*Facing, bottom:*
**9. WREXHAM, 1961**

GWR 'Manor' Class 4-6-0 7817 *Garsington Manor* passing through Wrexham General station with a southbound mixed freight during April 1961.The distinctive station buildings have fortunately been retained and restored in recent years.
*[R. W. Hinton]*

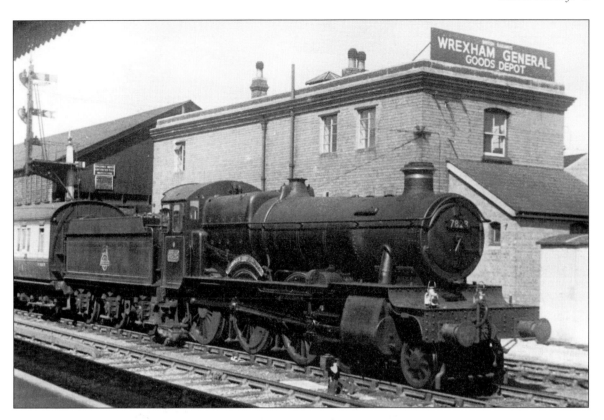

**10. WREXHAM, 2005**

In a view that has changed little from that taken over forty years earlier, a Class 47 diesel heads a special train at Wrexham General. Although the train carries the livery of Virgin Trains the locomotive had by then transferred to Freightliner and the rolling stock had joined the Riviera Trains fleet. The date is 10 April 2005 and the occasion was the LDV Vans Trophy final at Cardiff's Millennium Stadium. Wrexham beat Southend 2-0. *[George Jones]*

**11. WREXHAM, 2005**

An experimental freight train comprising seven OTA wagons topped and tailed by German-built Multi Purpose Vehicles (MPV) on loan from Network Rail arriving at Wrexham General. After loading with timber at Aberystwyth, the train departed around midday and arrived at Wrexham mid-afternoon before reversing and heading for the Kronospan siding at Chirk to unload. Trial workings were generally punctual but the concept has not been adopted, probably due to the difficulty in obtaining funding for the MPV units. *[George Jones]*

**12. WREXHAM, 1967**
Wrexham South Signal Box was situated south of the bridge which carries Regent Street across Wrexham General station and opposite the end of the up side bay platforms. The point in the foreground gives access to the loop line at the back face of the down island platform. 4 March 1967.
*[A. O. Wynn]*

# Main Line from Rossett to Gresford Bank

**13. ROSSETT, *c*.1900**

A view of Rossett looking towards Chester showing the substantial station building on the Up side with a smaller building on the Down platform which also boasts a good collection of luggage barrows. The uniformed figure outside the main building is probably the Station Master. *[Authors' Collection]*

**14. ROSSETT, *c*.1900**
A passenger's eye view from the Up platform looking towards Wrexham. The station was closed by BR in 1964. The considerable increase in housing in the area in recent years has resulted in much pressure to re-open the station, so far without success.
[*W. Alister Williams Collection*]

**15. ROSSETT, *c*.1929**
Rossett Sand & Gravels Ltd was served by a siding off the Shrewsbury & Chester line at Rossett. Rail traffic ceased when the pits closed in 1948 and was not resumed when the site was reopened in 1952 by the United Gravel Company Ltd. A number of GWR and LMS wagons can be identified in this late 1920s view. [*S. A. Weatherley Collection*]

**16. GRESFORD, c.1989**

A view taken during the construction of a new railway bridge over the A483 Marford bypass. The line between Wrexham and Saltney Junction had been singled in 1986 as a cost cutting measure since traffic levels at that time were in decline. The line is seen slewed on a temporary formation to allow construction of the bridge. It is ironic that the singling is now a serious constraint and a recent study has proposed redoubling the section of the line between the two points at which the A483 crosses the line. [*Dave Southern*]

**17. GRESFORD, c.1950**

The fireman of GWR 2-8-0 3801 is probably working hard as she blasts up Gresford Bank with a mixed freight train. Note the tarpaulin covers over some of the vans, no doubt to protect vulnerable loads. [*C. E. Stephens*]

## 18. GRESFORD, *c*.1950

GWR 2-6-0 5353 passing Gresford station with a Chester bound freight. The line in this area was heavily affected by mining subsidence and a 40 mph speed restriction applied to all trains. The large amounts of ash visible between the tracks were dropped by the Permanent Way Dept. in an attempt to stabilise the trackbed. The siding visible on the left was used to divide a train which had insufficient power to reach the summit. With a capacity of 68 wagons, as many as possible would be placed in the siding and the remainder of the train would proceed forward to Wrexham. Gresford would then arrange for the recessed wagons to be cleared as soon as practicable. An interesting feature to working the siding was provision of a shunting gong to inform the drivers of freight trains when it was safe to set back. The gong was attached to a telegraph pole ahead of the Up advanced starting signal and was operated by the guard by means of a plunger on the Chester end of the Up platform. *[C. E. Stephens]*

**19. GRESFORD, 1965**

In this view, looking towards Chester, the GWR standard pattern of timber box can be seen controlling access to the Colliery sidings. This type of box was used in unstable ground situations as evidenced by the spoil heaps to the rear. Note the conveyor crossing the line which conveyed the spoil from the Colliery on the right to the tip site.

*[R. S. Carpenter – P. J. Garland collection]*

*Facing page*

**20. GRESFORD, *c*.1970**

A typical industrial railway scene at Gresford Colliery showing a Hunslet Austerity Class 0-6-0ST surrounded by pools of water and coal slurry. One of the worst disasters in British mining history occurred here on 22 September 1934 when 260 men lost their lives. The pit closed in 1973 due to geological problems. *[E. N. Kneale]*

Access to Gresford Colliery was controlled by the United Colliery Signal Box. Down trains of empty wagons ran into A or F and then set back into B or E while up trains ran into B or E and then set back into A or F. The wagons were then worked to C, through the screens for loading and into J before being moved to H from where they were gravitated into A or F ready for collection.

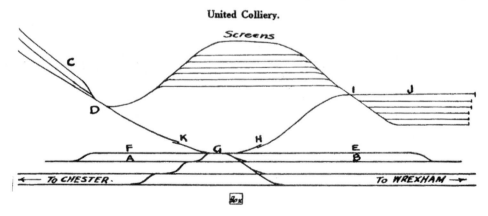

# Wrexham's Engine Sheds

## Introduction

Wrexham once had three main line engine sheds; Croes Newydd serving the Great Western, Rhosddu providing for the Wrexham, Mold & Connah's Quay line and Wrexham Central for the Cambrian line to Ellesmere. All three are now closed but during 2008 a new servicing depot was constructed in the disused south-facing bay platforms at Wrexham General for servicing the rolling stock used on the Wrexham & Shropshire Railway's new service to London Marylebone.

## Croes Newydd

Wrexham (Croes Newydd) locomotive shed was the last of the 'northlight' design of roundhouse sheds built by the Great Western Railway and was opened in 1902, replacing outdated facilities at Wheatsheaf Junction. Whilst the roundhouse style particularly suited the location, bounded as it was between the North and South forks of the Brymbo Branch and the Shrewsbury & Chester main line, this type of shed was not especially favoured by the operating staff as it relied on 100% efficiency of the turntable giving access to and from the locomotive storage roads.

Whilst in theory the 'northlight' roof offered maximum daylight into the building, in practice roof lights in a smoky engine shed quickly became encrusted with soot. As a result conditions within the shed, whilst offering a magical charm to the railway enthusiast who might occasionally enter surreptitiously or even with permission, presented those responsible for maintaining and preparing the locomotives housed there with a much less attractive working environment. In particular, the fitters who strove to maintain the shed's fleet faced conditions which today would be condemned as hazardous, if not outright dangerous.

The engines based at Croes Newydd were mostly of classes regarded as workhorses, as illustrated by the final GWR allocation list prior to nationalisation, as compiled on 31 December 1947:

| | |
|---|---|
| 'Manor' Class 4-6-0 | 7817 *Garsington Manor* |
| 'WD' Class 2-8-0 | WD 70808 (BR 90315), WD 78714 (BR 90656) |
| 'ROD' Class 2-8-0 | 3026, 3028 |
| '43xx' Class 2-6-0 | 4375, 5315, 5319, 5334, 5365, 6303, 6316, 6327, 7305, 7310 |
| '2251' Class 0-6-0 | 2227, 2259, 2287, 3203, 3206 |
| '66xx' Class 0-6-2T | 6694, 6698 |

Various Classes of 0-6-0PT   1532, 1747, 1780, 2183, 2188, 2190, 2704, 2716,  2717,
                             2744, 9656
'14xx' Class 0-4-2T          1401, 1411, 1416, 1428, 1457

Unsurprisingly the ubiquitous Pannier Tanks predominate, being well suited to the shunting and pick-up freight duties associated with the industrial nature of the district, as well as putting in sterling service on passenger duties to destinations as far away as Bala. The 2-6-0 and 0-6-0 types were solid mixed traffic locomotives, capable of working passenger and freight trains through to the Cambrian Coast, Chester, Shrewsbury and beyond. The two types of heavy freight 2-8-0s are examples of the standard military types of the two World Wars and which gave many years of service on the main line after the conflicts were over. The delightful little Collett 0-4-2Ts were designed specifically for push-pull passenger services such as those to Ellesmere and Llangollen. The sole named engine, the relatively new *Garsington Manor*, probably worked the principal services of the day to and from Barmouth.

The pictures of the shed in this book set out to portray the working atmosphere of a busy motive power depot in the closing years of steam on British Railways. By this time the steam locomotives depicted were nearing the end of their working lives and were often very unkempt in appearance. The ensuing years since 1947 had seen many changes, including transfer of the surviving lines in the Wrexham area from the Western Region to the London Midland Region of British Railways in 1963. As a result there was an influx of former LMS and BR Standard types, which the former Great Western men tended to lump together and refer to disparagingly as 'Midland' engines. The former military 2-8-0s were replaced by GWR Churchward and Collett 2-8-0s of the '28xx' and '38xx' Classes, followed by LMS Stanier '8F' 2-8-0s which made some impressive appearances on the Brymbo branch following their grudging acceptance by Croes Newydd's drivers. The ultimate in British steam locomotives arrived in 1965 in the form of the BR Standard '9F' 2-10-0. However, as at a number of other sheds around the country, the crews did not have the opportunity to exploit their full potential as Croes Newydd closed in March 1967 and the locomotives were dispersed, either immediately to the scrapyard or to another shed to give a few more months' service before withdrawal.

### Rhosddu

The history of Wrexham's other main shed is altogether different. In the pioneering days of the WM&CQ the locomotive arrangements by necessity displayed a distinct air of 'make do and mend', the only drawback being that for several years the company did not even possess a building in which to even do that! However, by 1874, when only three of the company's eight

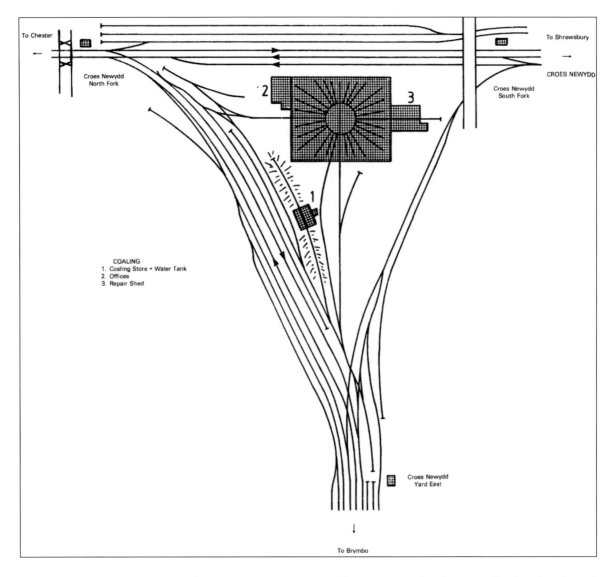

To Chester

Croes Newydd
North Fork

To Shrewsbury

CROES NEWYDD

Croes Newydd
South Fork

2

3

1

COALING
1. Coaling Store + Water Tank
2. Offices
3. Repair Shed

Croes Newydd
Yard East

To Brymbo

locomotives were serviceable, it was resolved to remedy the situation. A fitting shop was commissioned and this opened in 1876, becoming the nucleus of Rhosddu Works. A wooden locomotive running shed was subsequently erected but was blown down in a gale about 1910. It was replaced by a permanent brick structure in 1912, by which time the Great Central Railway was in charge and locomotive policy was directed from Gorton Works in Manchester. However, the relative remoteness of Rhosddu continued to be capitalised upon by local staff and stories of unorthodox practices are legion. A degree of autonomy continued through the LNER years until ultimately the London Midland Region took control in the 1950s before Rhosddu closed in 1962.

## Wrexham Central

Although the Cambrian did on occasion use Rhosddu, it also had a shed on the south side of the line just west of Wrexham Central. It was opened with the Ellesmere line in 1895 and for a time two of the Cambrian's Nasmyth Wilson 0-4-4T locomotives, as illustrated on the cover and frontispiece of this book, were based there. The shed closed in 1925 following the absorption of the Cambrian by the GWR and was dismantled and moved to Aberaeron in 1926.

## Cudworth & Johnson

Cudworth & Johnson were a firm of locomotive engineers, dealers and hirers. The company's headquarters was the Eagle Foundry in Wrexham and it also had a workshop at Rhosddu where heavy locomotive repairs took place. It is understood that in the early decades of the twentieth century there was often close co-operation between this workshop and the nearby WM&CQ works.

**21. LLAY HALL, *c*.1955**

Occasionally locomotives owned by the firm were stored at other locations in the Wrexham area between hires. For example, *Deptford*, a Black Hawthorn 0-4-0T works number 1038 of 1893, was stored at Llay Hall on two occasions during the 1950s. *[Industrial Locomotive Society– Frank Jones Collection]*

**22. CROES NEWYDD, 1965**
Croes Newydd North Fork signal box was built by the GWR in 1905 and housed a frame of 83 levers. It controlled the junction of the Brymbo branch with the main line, several sidings and a loop line to South Fork as well as a level crossing. The line in the foreground is the shed road while the next two are the Brymbo branch. Resignalling schemes undertaken between 1986 and 1988 left North Fork as the only remaining signal box in the Wrexham area. *[A. O. Wynn]*

**23. CROES NEWYDD, *c*.1963**
GWR 2-8-0 3817 on the Down Main line at North Fork. It will probably reverse here to gain access to Croes Newydd engine shed. *[E. N. Kneale]*

**24. CROES NEWYDD, *c*.1965**
An unidentified GWR 0-6-2T of the
66xx Class is seen on the turntable
within the shed from which the
radiating locomotive storage roads
can be clearly seen. The
importance, and vulnerability, of
the turntable in the operation of a
roundhouse shed is well illustrated.
*[E. N. Kneale]*

**25. CROES NEWYDD, *c*.1965**
A shaft of sunlight illuminates
GWR 2-8-0 3855 as it stands
alongside the turntable.
*[E. N. Kneale]*

**26. CROES NEWYDD, *c*.1965**
A cheery group of shed staff pose
alongside 3855. *[E. N. Kneale]*

**27. CROES NEWYDD, *c*.1965**
The piles of ash & clinker surrounding GWR 0-6-2T 6651 graphically illustrate the dirt and grime associated with a locomotive shed in the final years of steam working. *[E. N. Kneale]*

**28. CROES NEWYDD, *c*.1965**
GWR 0-6-0PT 9630 stands under the coaling stage where things seem relatively tidy compared to the previous scene.
*[E. N. Kneale]*

**29. CROES NEWYDD, 1965**

Former LMS locomotives together with BR Standard types dominate this view taken from the turntable. *[E. N. Kneale]*

**30. CROES NEWYDD, *c*.1965**
A young enthusiast, notebook in hand, looks over BR 'Standard' Class 4 4-6-0 75026 in Croes Newydd yard. Access was privileged, his father being a Fireman here. The young man is now the Chief Mechanical Engineer of the Llangollen Railway.
*[Ivor Owen]*

**31. CROES NEWYDD, 1965**

GWR 0-6-0PT 1358 enters Croes Newydd yard via the single track curve from Croes Newydd South Fork. Glimpses of at least five different locomotives 'on shed' may be seen in the background. 9 March 1965. [*Brian Cowlishaw*]

### 32. CROES NEWYDD YARD, 1959

Croes Newydd East signal box and its impressive bracket signal are the main features in this view of Croes Newydd yard looking towards Croes Newydd West and Brymbo. The signal was later replaced by two separate signals, one for each direction. The replacements were of Western Region standard tubular post design. *[R. S. Carpenter – P. J. Garland collection]*

### 33. CROES NEWYDD YARD, 1956 (below)

Staff at Croes Newydd Yard gather for an informal photograph. The Yard Master (with braid on the peak of his cap) and four of his staff chat with the crew of GWR 2-6-0 5328. *[Wrexham Leader]*

### 34. CROES NEWYDD YARD, 1965

*(below)*

A GWR '56xx' 0-6-2T stands in Croes Newydd Yard with two brake vans during a pause in shunting. The shunter, complete with pole, is walking towards the coal wagons on the right of the picture to prepare for the next move. *[J. F. A. Hobbs]*

**35. CROES NEWYDD YARD, 1965**

A GWR '38xx' 2-8-0 sets back onto its train at the west end of Croes Newydd yard. The train is destined for Brymbo steelworks and conveys a number of coke wagons. 9 March 1965. *[Brian Cowlishaw]*

**36. CROES NEWYDD YARD, 1965**

Another freight departs for Brymbo on the same day, this time with a 38xx as banker. Croes Newydd West box is on the left while the building on the right houses the weighbridge, yard master's, goods clerks and goods agent's offices. The signal box was re-sited at some point in its history as 1925 plans show it on the opposite side of the line and behind the road bridge from which this photograph was taken. *[Brian Cowlishaw]*

**37. CROES NEWYDD YARD, 1979**

The same location fourteen years later shows a dramatic decline with only a few wagons visible. Sidings have been lifted and most of the buildings have disappeared. Class 46 diesel locomotive 46034 returns 'light engine' after presumably arriving with a freight train. [*Trefor Thompson*]

# Wrexham to Ruabon

**38. WREXHAM, 1976**

Class 25 25290 departs from Wrexham on 12 July 1976 with a southbound parcels train. To the right another Class 25 is shunting in Watery Road goods yard. In the left background can be seen Croes Newydd North Fork signal box. The white building on the extreme left is the drivers' signing-on point, erected after closure of the steam shed. *[Tom Heavyside]*

**39. WREXHAM, 1965**

Class 40 D342 passes Croes Newydd South Fork with a coal train. The signals on the right are a former GWR type fitted with route indicators. Note the associated cranks and balance levers. *[E. N. Kneale]*

**40. BERSHAM, 1972**

A busy scene at Bersham as Class 25 D5280 propels empty wagons into the colliery siding. The colliery locomotive *Hornet* waits on the left to take over after the BR loco has left. Also of note are the permanent way gang carrying out maintenance on the Up main line. Bersham was one of the smaller pits in the Wrexham area but was the last to close, surviving until December 1986. *[Tom Heavyside]*

**41. BERSHAM, *c*.1978**
A close up view of 0-4-0ST *Hornet* shunting wagons into the colliery yard. *Hornet* was built in 1937 by Peckett of Bristol, works number 1935. *[Dave Southern]*

**42. JOHNSTOWN, *c*.1960**
Johnstown & Hafod station was opened in 1896, 48 years after the opening of the Shrewsbury & Chester line. It became an unstaffed halt on 1 June 1955 and closed to all traffic except that from Hafod Colliery on 12 September 1960. *[Denbighshire Record Office]*

**43. HAFOD, *c*.1957**

Hafod Colliery was served by sidings on the up side of the Shrewsbury & Chester line just north of Johnstown & Hafod station. An interesting locomotive which worked at Hafod between 1934 and 1961 was this 0-6-0T built by the North British Locomotive Company as works number 21521 of 1917. Originally built for the Glasgow & South Western Railway, the locomotive was sold out of service by the LMS in 1934. After its colliery career it was stored for a while at Oswestry Works before being returned to Glasgow for preservation. *[Frank Jones]*

**44. HAFOD, 1965**

Hafod Brickworks was owned by the famous brick making firm of Dennis (Ruabon) Ltd and was situated to the east of the Shrewsbury & Chester line. It was served by a standard gauge siding from the Hafod Colliery system while a double track 1' 9¹/₂" gauge tramway with overhead rope haulage was used to bring clay from the pit to the brickworks. This view shows a train of loaded wagons on their way from the clay pit to the brickworks. *[P. G. Hindley]*

**45. RUABON, 1957**

A pair of GWR 'Dukedog' Class 4-4-0s, with 9018 leading, prepare to leave Ruabon with a Ffestiniog Railway Society special for Porthmadog. Such specials, originating in London and travelling either via Machynlleth or Dolgellau, were a feature of the early years of the preservation era on the Ffestiniog Railway and often brought interesting motive power to Ruabon. [*A. O. Wynn*]

**46. RUABON, *c*.1964**
LMS 'Black Five' 4-6-0 45004 takes water at Ruabon while working a Chester to Shrewsbury parcels train formed of a mix of LMS and BR standard vans. [*A. O. Wynn*]

**47. RUABON, 1957**

GWR 0-6-2T 6694 passes Ruabon with a southbound train of steel pipes on 13 June 1957. The importance of freight traffic to British Railways in general, and Ruabon in particular, in the 1950s is emphasised in this picture. Two northbound freights may be seen behind 6694's train and a large number of wagons are stabled in the area awaiting their next loads. [*R. W. Hinton*]

**48. RUABON, 1964**

An example of the unusual motive power which worked to Ruabon on FRS specials was former Southern Railway 'Battle of Britain' Class 4-6-2 34064 *Fighter Command*. It is seen here standing at the south end of the bay platform, its train having already been taken forward to Porthmadog via Llangollen, Dolgellau and Barmouth. *[A. O. Wynn]*

**49. RUABON, 1953**

Station staff at Ruabon after the passage of the Royal Train conveying Her Majesty the Queen to Llangollen. *[A. Cliff]*

**50. RUABON,** *c.1950*

Arriving on the Up main platform is GWR 0-6-0PT 9621 on a local stopping train. The majority of the waiting passengers appear to be lady shoppers.

*[J. Roberts Collection – Courtesy of P. Fisher]*

**51. RUABON SOUTH, *c*.1965**
Ruabon was originally a marshalling point for the trip workings serving local branch lines, collieries, brickworks and other industries. It was served by three signal boxes, North, Middle & South, the third of which is seen here being passed by a mixed freight hauled by Class 47 diesel D1865. *[J. Roberts Collection – Courtesy of P. Fisher]*

**52. RUABON SOUTH, *c*.1960**
The size of the lever frame in Ruabon South signal box belies its exterior dimensions. It appears to have been built with future expansion in mind, which did not happen. Note the emblematic signalman's duster on the reversed lever. *[J. Roberts Collection – Courtesy of P. Fisher]*

**53. RUABON SOUTH, *c*.1960**
Once the exclusive preserve of GWR locomotives, after nationalisation former LMS engines became a more familiar sight. Here an LMS 'Crab' 2-6-0 passes the site of the former Wynnstay Colliery with a short mixed freight. These engines were built at the former Lancashire & Yorkshire railway works at Horwich. *[J. Roberts Collection – Courtesy of P. Fisher]*

**54. RUABON, 1965**
LMS Stanier '8F' 2-8-0 48747 passing Llangollen Line Junction, 54 chains south of Ruabon station, during 1965. The Llangollen line closed to passengers on 18 January 1965 and to freight on 1 April 1968. *[A. O. Wynn]*

**55. RHOSYMEDRE, *c*.1910**
Rhosymedre Halt, built by the GWR for the use of miners and workmen, was opened on 1 September 1906 and closed on 2 March 1959. *[Lens of Sutton]*

**56. CEFN, *c*.1960**
Cefn station was situated near the north end of Cefn Viaduct and was provided with a signal box which controlled access to two private sidings. Like many of the other smaller stations on the Shrewsbury & Chester line, Cefn was closed on 12 September 1960. *[Denbighshire Record Office]*

**57. CEFN VIADUCT, 1984**

The viaduct over the Dee at Cefn has 19 stone arches each with a span of 60 feet. It is 1508 feet long and 147 feet high. The structure cost £72,346 to construct and was completed in two years. Mr Ormsby-Gore, Chairman of the Shrewsbury & Chester Railway, described the structure designed by Henry Robertson and built by Thomas Brassey as 'an extraordinary triumph of art over the difficulties of Nature.' Seen crossing in this view is a steam special hauled by former Southern Railway Pacific 35028 *Clan Line* of the 'Merchant Navy' Class. *[Tom Heavyside]*

**58. PENYBONT SIDING, *c*.1956**

J. C. Edwards obtained this 40hp four wheeled petrol engined locomotive new in 1919 from Motor Rail of Bedford, who allocated it their works number 1922. For the next forty years it saw regular use hauling the products of Penybont brickworks from the loading bank seen here to the junction with the Shrewsbury to Chester main line where they were collected by the local pick-up goods train for onward distribution. It was scrapped early in 1961 during the demolition of the works following closure the previous year. A number of similar locomotives worked at other locations in Denbighshire and Flintshire and one has survived in private preservation at a location near Mold. *[C. H. A. Townley – J. Thomas Collection]*

## 59. FRON BRANCH, 1956

South of Cefn Viaduct two short industrial branches left the Shrewsbury & Chester line at Fron Branch Junction, the Fron Branch to Chirk Castle Lime Works on the down side and J C Edwards' Penybont Siding on the up side. Wagons from the main line for the three quarter mile long Fron Branch were left in an 11 wagon loop just inside the gate at Fron Branch Junction from where a contractor worked them on to the Lime Works, in 1925 his fee was 4 shillings (20p) per wagon. The contractor used horse power because there was a low bridge under the Shropshire Union Canal to be negotiated and the final access to the Lime Works was via wagon turntables, both of which prevented the use of locomotives. Traffic for J C Edwards' was propelled into the Penybont Siding and secured behind a gate from where it was collected by the company's locomotive for transfer to the brick and tile works. Outward traffic from the works was returned to the gate for collection. The siding gate with wagons behind it may be seen on the right of this photograph of GWR 2-6-0 9304 heading south with a van train on 6 August 1956. Penybont Siding remained in use until the closure of J. C. Edwards' works in 1960. *[R. W. Hinton]*

**60. WHITEHURST, *c*.1960**

A view of the yard at Whitehurst which once had siding space for 130 wagons, a cattle dock, a 20 ton wagon weighbridge and the warehouse visible in the distance. The yard, which closed on 10 June 1963, was the marshalling point for traffic to and from the Fron Branch and Penybont Siding. In the early days of the railway, and before the line to Llangollen opened, the building in the foreground was part of 'Llangollen Road' station. *[Denbighshire Record Office]*

**61. CHIRK, 1963**

Chirk station remains open to passengers but closed to freight on 13 July 1964. In this view looking south the main station buildings can be seen. Efforts to preserve them as being of architectural interest were unsuccessful and they were demolished in 1987. *[M. A. King]*

**62. CHIRK,** *c.*1950

A view of the yard and signal box as GWR 'Hall' Class 4-6-0 6901 *Arley Hall* passes on a Paddington bound express. *[R. Stephens]*

**63. CHIRK, 1989**

By 1989 Chirk passenger station had become an unstaffed halt but freight traffic was enjoying a renaissance thanks to the nearby Kronospan chipboard factory. Initially raw timber was brought from railheads in East Anglia via Warrington (Walton Old Junction) although it now comes primarily from Scotland. Class 31 diesel 31242 is departing for Warrington with two empty OTA timber wagons. *[Paul Shannon]*

**64. WESTON RHYN, 1989**

Another view of 31242 with the two empty OTA wagons. Because there are no run round facilities at Chirk, empty trains are booked to travel to Gobowen to run round before returning north. However, prior to the closure of the signal box at Weston Rhyn on 4 April 1991 the manoeuvre was often accomplished here instead. Llangollen Railway volunteers removed the signal box on 4 August 1991 and it is currently stored at Carrog awaiting re-use. The passenger station here, known as Preesgweene until February 1935, closed in 1960. *[Paul Shannon]*

**65. WESTON RHYN, 1966**
In this view the extensive facilities for the marshalling of traffic to and from Ifton Colliery can be seen beyond the railway's boundary fence. [*C. H. A. Townley*]

**66. WESTON RHYN, *c.*1991**
The Shrewsbury to Chester line has become a popular venue for steam hauled special trains. Here LMS 'Princess Royal Pacific' 4-6-2 6201 *Princess Elizabeth* makes a splendid sight as it pounds through Weston Rhyn. [*E. N. Kneale*]

**67. GOBOWEN, *c*.1860**

Gobowen was the junction for the Shrewsbury & Chester Railway's short branch to Oswestry.
This fine view, taken at the north end of Gobowen station, shows the Italianate style station
building and the timber trainshed over the Oswestry branch platform beyond. The period dress
of the railway staff and their families is also of interest. [*Shropshire Records & Research Unit*]

**68. GOBOWEN, 1998**

The modern diesel age arrives with a Shrewsbury bound two-car DMU of the 175 'Coradia' Class. [*George Jones*]

**69. GOBOWEN, 2007**

Class 67 67029 approaches Gobowen on 13 June 2007 with EWS Railway's executive train on a route proving run for Wrexham & Shropshire Railway's Wrexham to London service.   *[George Jones]*

# Lines to Brymbo

## Development of the System

A lorry driver delivering materials to Brymbo Steelworks in the 1980s had to negotiate a series of narrow, twisting roads and steep gradients on the last stage of his journey to the works high in the hills above Wrexham. One driver, on arriving at the works, is said to have remarked, "Why on earth did you build a steelworks on top of a &*!% hill?" It was of course the presence of suitable raw materials; namely iron ore, coal and limestone which encouraged the Ironmasters to set up at Brymbo in the early nineteenth century. It was likewise the possibility of transporting these materials to the markets of Merseyside and beyond which encouraged several railways to promote lines into this relatively small area.

The first line to Brymbo was a branch of the North Wales Mineral Railway opened in July 1847 from Wheatsheaf Junction across the Moss Valley to Brymbo and Minera. The line served Brymbo Ironworks as well as the limestone quarry and lead mine at Minera. A short branch from Brymbo to Vron Colliery opened in November 1847 together with a line down the valley to serve Southsea Colliery at Broughton. Coal from this pit had perhaps the most circuitous route of all, travelling up the valley to Brymbo where a reversal was necessary to gain the system of inclines through the Moss Valley before the Shrewsbury & Chester line was finally reached at Wheatsheaf Junction.

The next railway built in the area did not immediately reach Brymbo and was built by a company one would not associate with the Wrexham area, the Chester & Holyhead. This company bought the Mold Railway to ensure the completion of that company's line from Saltney Ferry (later Mold Junction) to Mold. Part of the Act for the construction of that line also gave powers for a branch from Padeswood to Ffrith to serve the limeworks there. Following the opening of the line to Mold in August 1849, the first $2\frac{1}{4}$ miles of the branch to Coed Talon were opened in September 1849. This branch was later extended to Llanfynydd where it made an end-on junction with the Wrexham & Minera Extension Railway. At Coed Talon the branch served Nerquis Colliery which had its own private railway from the pit head. Several other collieries opened at Coed Talon and Leeswood in the 1860s and the Coppa Oil Company was established to extract oil from the locally mined 'cannel' coal. The additional traffic which developed necessitated the doubling of the Coppa to Ffrith Junction section in 1866.

The next railway to enter the valley was the Wrexham & Minera, a $3\frac{1}{4}$ mile branch from Croes Newydd to Brymbo to join the NWMR branch to Minera. This was opened on 22 May 1862 and allowed the western incline

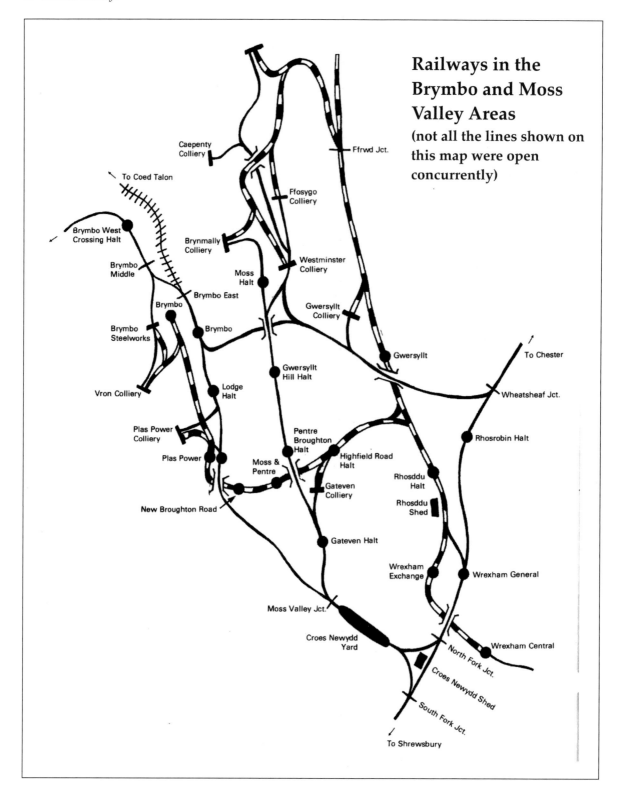

**Railways in the Brymbo and Moss Valley Areas**
(not all the lines shown on this map were open concurrently)

To Coed Talon

Caepenty Colliery

Ffrwd Jct.

Brymbo West Crossing Halt

Ffosygo Colliery

Brynmally Colliery

Brymbo Middle

Westminster Colliery

Moss Halt

Brymbo East

Gwersyllt Colliery

Brymbo

Brymbo Steelworks

Brymbo

Gwersyllt

To Chester

Gwersyllt Hill Halt

Wheatsheaf Jct.

Vron Colliery

Lodge Halt

Rhosrobin Halt

Plas Power Colliery

Pentre Broughton Halt

Highfield Road Halt

Plas Power

Moss & Pentre

Rhosddu Halt

Gateven Colliery

Rhosddu Shed

New Broughton Road

Gateven Halt

Wrexham Exchange

Wrexham General

Moss Valley Jct.

Croes Newydd Yard

North Fork Jct.

Wrexham Central

Croes Newydd Shed

South Fork Jct.

To Shrewsbury

of the old line from Wheatsheaf Junction to be closed, the new line providing a shorter and more easily worked route between Wrexham and Brymbo. Only part of the line was completely new as between Broughton & Brymbo it incorporated the original NWMR Southsea branch.

Returning to Coed Talon, in the 1860s the output of the collieries was steadily expanding with up to nine trains a day passing onto the Ffrith branch via the Nerquis Railway. The volume of traffic combined with the steep gradients on the branch caused the LNWR, who had absorbed the C&H, to promote a Bill to purchase the Nerquis Railway with a view towards extending it to Mold. The line was transferred to the LNWR in 1868 and was completely rebuilt and extended northwards to join the existing Mold Junction to Mold line just south of the town at Tryddyn Junction. The new line was opened for goods traffic on 8 July 1870. However, the connection to Nerquis Colliery was removed in 1887 and the line appears to have been disused until the commencement of passenger services between Mold and Coed Talon in 1892. The colliery connection was reinstated in 1923.

The next stage of development was fairly obvious, to link Brymbo and Coed Talon to create a through route between Wrexham and Mold. The Wrexham & Minera obtained powers in 1865 for an extension from Brymbo to join the Ffrith branch at Tryddyn, south of Coed Talon. This extension was leased jointly to the LNWR and GWR in 1866 and became known as the Wrexham & Minera Extension Joint Railway. The 2³/₄ mile branch was opened on 27 January 1872, the LNWR having completed the southern section of the Ffrith branch at the same time.

The final piece of this complex jigsaw was added as the Wrexham, Mold & Connah's Quay Railway sought a share of the Brymbo traffic and, despite opposition from the GWR, it obtained an Act in August 1882 to build a branch from a junction on its main line near Gwersyllt. This was opened in stages; Brymbo Junction to Moss & Pentre in 1882, Moss & Pentre to Plas Power in 1884 and Plas Power to Brymbo in December 1887. A short branch from Brymbo to Vron Colliery was opened on 8 October 1888. This branch was at a lower level than the GWR branch which it joined just before the Colliery.

The railway map of Brymbo was now complete giving this small area lines which approached from three different directions and were built by six different companies. Changes in ownership saw the Wrexham & Minera and North Wales Mineral become part of the GWR, the C&H become part of the LNWR and then the LMS while the WM&CQ became part of the GCR and then the LNER. Therefore at the Grouping in 1923 three of the Big Four railways were competing for the traffic from Brymbo.

*This plan shows the complicated track layout around Broughton Forge and Broughton Crossing signal boxes as it was in 1925. Broughton Forge had a connection to Broughton Solvay Coke Ovens as well as the transfer siding with the LNER (previously GCR) and Plas Power. Both the LNER and the Broughton & Plas Power Coal Company contributed towards the operating costs. At Broughton Crossing there was a connection to the Broughton & Plas Power Coal Company locomotive shed; colliery locomotives were permitted to travel over the GWR line between the two signal boxes as required.*

### Passenger Services

Although the lines to Brymbo were built for mineral use some passenger services were also operated. The shortest lived service was on the WM&CQ which commenced on 1 August 1889 and was withdrawn on 1 March 1917. The reason for the poor patronage of the service is not hard to find; the route was over a mile longer than the rival GWR route, it passed through mainly rural areas and its Brymbo terminus was inconveniently situated below the village. The GCR even ran steam railmotors on the branch to try and encourage passengers but without success, the rival bus services which had started up in the area proving more attractive.

The GWR service cannot be said to have been much more successful but Paddington, having more resources (and perhaps being more stubborn) persevered for longer. The service between Wrexham General and Brymbo started on 24 May 1882 and was extended to Coed Poeth in 1897 and Berwig in 1905. Like the GC the GWR also ran railmotors in an attempt to compete with road transport but with no more success. Defeat was finally admitted with the withdrawal of the service on 1 January 1931.

The longest lived service was that between Brymbo and Mold operated by the LNWR and then the LMS. It commenced between Mold and Coed Talon on 1 January 1892 and was extended to Brymbo on 15 November 1897. The service became the only one to survive into the British Railways era, being withdrawn on 27 March 1950.

### Closure and Abandonment

The closure of the lines to Brymbo, like their opening, was a piecemeal affair with sections closing as the mineral deposits were worked out and the mines and quarries became uneconomic.

The first line to close was the Ffrith branch which, as previously mentioned, had never had a passenger service and consequently received only minimal maintenance which resulted in the derailment of a goods train on 27 September 1934. As most of the traffic to Coed Talon now passed via Tryddyn Junction it was not considered worthwhile to repair the Ffrith branch and it was abandoned.

The Tryddyn Junction to Brymbo line survived into the BR era before being closed in three sections. First to be closed was the central section between  Coed Talon and Bwlchgwyn Siding on 1 January 1951. The two end sections survived for another 12 years before closing within a few months of each other. Tryddyn Junction to Coed Talon retained a daily goods train until closure on 22 July 1963 while Brymbo to  Bwlchgwyn, which had been retained to serve a quarry, closed on 1 October 1963.

The GCR Brymbo branch also closed in three sections with the centre section going first. On 30 November 1954 a new connection between the GCR and GWR Brymbo branches was opened at Plas Power allowing the sections of the GCR branch between Plas Power and Gatewen to be closed. Lifting followed in 1958. This new connection, together with the Plas Power to Brymbo section and Vron branch, closed on 19 June 1958 but was then reopened on 1 May 1965 for five more years use before final closure on 5 October 1970. The Brymbo Junction to Gatewen section, which latterly served the NCBOE Gatewen Disposal Point, closed on 14 March 1960.

Thus the start of the 1970s saw the GWR line from Wrexham through Brymbo to Minera become the sole survivor of a once extensive system. The Brymbo to Minera section had not long to go, however, with closure occurring on 1 January 1972. The Wrexham to Brymbo line seemed to have a much more secure future than the rest of the system as it was still conveying a large quantity of traffic for the steelworks, both raw materials inward and finished product outward. With up to eight trains per day traversing the branch and poor road access to the works there seemed every reason to think that the line would remain open as long as the steelworks was in business. A reversal in its fortunes began with the dramatic events of the early part of 1980. On 1 January a national steel strike began and lasted for some three months. However, the dispute only involved the nationalised British Steel Corporation and private works, including Brymbo, operated normally. The railwaymen of Wrexham entered the dispute and decided to 'black' Brymbo as a gesture of support for the striking steelworkers. Although the blacking was lifted after two weeks it was long enough to allow road transport to capture a significant portion of the traffic. All raw materials were now coming in by road and all that was left for the railway was a daily trip to bring out that portion of the steel which had not been lost to the road hauliers, usually three or four wagons. By 1982 traffic had declined to only two or three trains per week and the inevitable closure occurred on 1 October. The last train actually ran on 29 September 1982 with two of the authors travelling in the brake van from Brymbo to Croes Newydd. Just one month later Croes Newydd yard also closed leaving the smaller Watery Road yard to cope with the remaining traffic, including some steel brought by road from Brymbo for onward carriage by rail.

This was not quite the end of Brymbo's railways, however, as the internal rail system of Brymbo Steelworks continued to operate after the closure of the branch. Ironically this incorporated part of the Vron branch, one of the original lines opened by the NWMR in 1847. In May 1990 the closure of Brymbo Steelworks was announced and steelmaking at Brymbo ceased in September of that year. The closure of the works and its internal rail system marked the end of railways in Brymbo after 143 years. However, track materials recovered from the works' internal system were re-used on the Llangollen Railway's westward extension to Glyndyfrdwy.

# Wrexham to Brymbo & Minera – GWR

### 70. PLAS POWER *c.*1910

Plas Power, 1 mile 65 chains from North Fork, was the first station on the branch. The staff may seem excessive for such a small station but according to the GWR it served the four villages of Southsea, Tan-y-fron, Adwy and New Broughton, which between them had a population of over 11,000. *[Arthur Jones]*

**71. BROUGHTON, 1965**

An unidentified English Electric Type 4 diesel passes Broughton Crossing Signal Box with a short trip working from Brymbo to Croes Newydd Yard on 13 March 1965. *[Brian Cowlishaw]*

**72. BRYMBO, 1965**

A typical Brymbo scene. In the shadow of the slag tips GWR '38xx' 2-8-0 3813 and an unidentified banker ease their train towards the site of Brymbo station. Some slag ladle wagons are visible in the top right of the picture while a classic Crosville bus completes the scene. June 1965. *[Brian Cowlishaw]*

**73. BRYMBO, *c*.1965**

LMS Stanier '8F' 2-8-0 48122 blackens the sky as it tackles the final leg of the journey to Brymbo Middle Signal Box.
*[A. O. Wynn]*

**74. BRYMBO, *c*.1905**

Lodge Halt was just 38 chains from Brymbo and comprised a basic wooden platform on each side of the line. A GWR Report in 1925 stated that a shelter was provided on each platform so presumably one was added on the Down platform after this picture was taken, The village of Lodge was a victim of the expansion of the steelworks and much of it was demolished in the 1960s and 1970s, the residents being rehoused by the steel company.  *[Pacer Archives]*

**75. BRYMBO,** *c.*1905

Brymbo station was 3 miles 9 chains from North Fork and was overshadowed by the steelworks on the hillside above it. It was inconvenient for the village, which was at a higher level, and so most passengers used the more convenient Brymbo West Halt. This view shows the station staff assembled in front of the wooden station buildings. Amongst the wealth of detail contained within the photograph are the single wheel platform barrow, the enamel advertisement signs and the oil lamps. Beyond the footbridge are the signal box and the station house. The bracket signal in front of the station house controlled the junction with the LMS line to Coed Talon and the LMS paid a proportion of the costs for the signal box.   [*Arthur Jones*]

**76. BRYMBO, 1952**

Although the passenger service had been withdrawn twenty-one years earlier the nameboard and station building were extant when this railtour run jointly by the Stephenson Locomotive Society and the Manchester Locomotive Society visited the branch. *[T. J. Edgington Collection]*

**77. BRYMBO, 1979**
A wintry scene as Class 25 25192 approaches Brymbo East with a train of empty wagons for the steelworks.
*[Trefor Thompson]*

**78. BRYMBO, *c*.1966**
The fireman of LMS '8F' 2-8-0 48665 leans casually out of his cab as he passes Brymbo East signal box whilst in charge of a freight bound for the steelworks. The building on the right is the former station house. *[A. O. Wynn]*

**79. BRYMBO, 1976**

Class 24 24063 leaves Brymbo for Croes Newydd Yard with a train of empty coke wagons and steel flats on 12 July 1976.
*[Tom Heavyside]*

**80. BRYMBO, 1965**

Brymbo Middle in 1965 with GWR '38xx' 2-8-0 3817 departing from the steelworks. The fireman is handing the train staff for the Vron branch to the signalman. The Vron branch passed through the steelworks to reach Vron Colliery. By the 1920s the GWR had ceased to serve the pit as it considered that the output 'did not warrant a service' and the remaining production departed via the GCR branch. After the GCR line closed in 1970 BR renamed the Vron branch Ty Cerreg Sidings.
*[J. F. A. Hobbs]*

**81. BRYMBO, 1965**

On arrival at Brymbo Middle Signal Box trains had to reverse to gain access to the steelworks via the Vron branch.
GWR 0-6-0PT 8709 is seen entering the works with a freight, which it had just banked from Croes Newydd.
*[A. O. Wynn]*

**82. BRYMBO, 1966**

In this view of former LMS '8F' 2-8-0 48252 reversing into the works the scale of the works site is well portrayed.
The other line off the main line where there are wagons standing was known as Warehouse siding.
*[C. H. A. Townley – R. W. Miller Collection]*

**83. BRYMBO, *c*.1955**

Brymbo Steelworks had its own fleet of locomotives operating on the internal railway system. *Gwynedd*, Black Hawthorn 1014 of 1890, spent its entire 67-year working life at the works.

*[Industrial Locomotive Society – Frank Jones Collection]*

**84. BRYMBO, 1957**

Versatile crane tank locomotives such as Brymbo's *Basic*, built by Dubs of Glasgow as their works number 2064 of 1884, were once a common sight in steelworks and shipyards. *Basic* spent its entire life at Brymbo, clocking up 74 years of service before being scrapped in 1958. *[J. Peden]*

**85. BRYMBO, 1957**

A relative youngster compared with *Basic*, *Sir Henry* was built by Robert Stephenson & Hawthorns of Newcastle in 1940 as their works number 7056. *Sir Henry*, named after Sir Henry Robertson, spent a year on loan to Foxfield Colliery in Staffordshire in 1946/7 and was scrapped in 1965 when its duties were taken over by diesel locomotives. *[J. Peden]*

**86. BRYMBO, 1957**

*Hope* was the second diesel locomotive to be introduced at Brymbo. Built by the Yorkshire Engine Co. of Sheffield as their works number 2632 of 1957, it was one of a batch of three 200 horsepower 0-6-0 diesel electrics purchased from the firm in 1957 after trials and subsequent purchase of a similar locomotive from the same builder in 1955. *Hope* was scrapped in 1983. *[J. Peden]*

**87. BRYMBO, *c*.1925**

A view of Brymbo West station looking towards Minera. The wooden platforms, station buildings and signal box are clearly shown. The line becomes single track beyond the level crossing. *[Authors' Collection]*

**88. CAELLO, 1962**

One of the main operating features of the line was the large number of level crossings, some of which were only yards apart. After leaving Brymbo four crossings - Caello, Smelt, Pentresaeson and Gegin - followed in quick succession. Under the GWR they were all manned but in BR days the gates had to be opened by the train crew, a tedious and time-consuming exercise. At Caello the line served a brick works and the photograph shows the horse drawn tramway, still operating in March 1962, which was used to transport clay to the works. *[M. E. M. Lloyd – H. J. Leadbetter Collection]*

**89. PENTRESAESON, 1967**

In the days when the branch had a passenger service there was a halt adjacent to the level crossing at Pentresaeson. It comprised a single wooden platform with a corrugated booking hut and shelter. It was normally unmanned but on Saturdays the level of traffic warranted a porter being sent from Wrexham General to book passengers. In this view BR Standard Class 4 2-6-0 76037 is leaving for Brymbo with a loaded mineral train. *[Brian Cowlishaw]*

**90. COEDPOETH, 1948**

Eighteen years after the end of passenger services this scene has hardly changed with station buildings and passing loop intact and all still looking neat and tidy. *[LGRP]*

**91. COEDPOETH, *c*.1965**
Compared with the previous view an air of neglect is now evident with the station building demolished and the loop line lifted. The signal box is still in situ but out of use and the signal is without an arm. The Brymbo to Minera section of line closed completely in 1972. *[Mike Lloyd / WRRC]*

**92. VICARAGE CROSSING, *c*.1960**
Vicarage Crossing was just 28 chains from Coed Poeth. It had a single platform on the down side of the line with a goods loop and loading bank on the up side. There was no signal box, the loop being controlled from two ground frames released by the train staff. In 1925 the crossing was operated by a gate woman who received a wage of 8 shillings (40p) a week. Most of the crossing keepers on the line were women, many of them being wives of railway employees. The photograph shows sidings beyond the loading bank which are thought to have been added after 1925 as they are not mentioned in the GWR report of that year. *[Hugh Davies]*

**93. BERWIG, c.1920**

Berwig Halt & Crossing was a mere 35 chains distant from Coed Poeth and was the terminus for passenger services on the line. The electric token system finished here, one engine in steam sufficing for the freight traffic onwards to Minera. In later years, following the withdrawal of passenger services, the entire line from Brymbo was worked one engine in steam. In spite of its close proximity to Vicarage Crossing, there was another level crossing at Cae Glas just 100 yards short of Berwig which was attended by the porter from Berwig who could be summoned by means of a bell. This 1920 view of Berwig clearly shows the crossing, halt and signal box. [*Arthur Jones*]

**94. MINERA LIME WORKS, *c*.1905**
From 1857 until their amalgamation in 1899, two companies had private sidings at Minera. Minera Lime Works sidings could hold 44 wagons while those of Lesters Lime Works could hold just three. The GWR provided a weighbridge while the Minera Lime Company had a water column for its own locomotive which the GWR was allowed to use. Traffic originating from Minera was always fairly light compared to Brymbo and a single shunter was considered sufficient to deal with it. *[John Ryan Collection]*

**95. MINERA, *c*.1900**
A track gang carrying out repairs to the sidings at Minera. Their style of dress is a considerable contrast with the safety and high visibility clothing requirements of their present day counterparts. *[Authors' Collection]*

**96. MINERA LIME WORKS, 1965**
An unidentified GWR 0-6-0PT shunts mineral wagons in the lime works sidings. The guard in his 1950s uniform rides on the
footplate, whilst the shunter is more casually dressed. *[Brian Taylor]*

**97. MINERA LIME WORKS, 1960**
Industrial locomotives were employed by the Minera Lime Company and its successor, Lythgoe Brothers. *Olwen* was new to Minera from Beyer, Peacock as works number 5408 in 1910 and remained at the works until scrapped in 1964.
*[Brian Cowlishaw]*

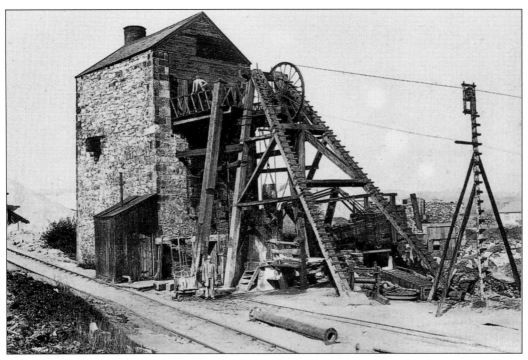

**98. NEW BRIGHTON, *c*.1905**
The Dellafield Lead Mines were located at New Brighton, approximately one mile from Minera, and were served by a private line. The mine closed in 1910 and the line was lifted only to be re-laid in the 1920s to serve the newly opened Silica Clay beds. In this view the original track can be seen running to the left of the City Shaft. *[Denbighshire Record Office]*

**99. MINERA, 1959**
GWR 0-6-OPTs 1635 and 1690 at Minera with an enthusiasts rail tour on 18 September 1959. The New Brighton branch can be seen climbing away at 1 in 30 above the rear coach. *[R. W. Miller]*

# Wrexham to Brymbo – The GCR Route

### 100. MOSS & PENTRE STATION, 1948

Many of the stations on this line remained in good condition despite the early demise of the passenger service, as can be seen in this view of a freight passing Moss & Pentre station in 1948. The name was not really appropriate as the station was at least a mile from the village of Moss, which was served more directly by the GWR Moss branch. It was really in the district of Broughton but the GWR already had Pentre Broughton Halt on their line. To complicate matters further, the next station on the GCR line was New Broughton Road. If all this confuses you then think of the poor traveller in the early 1900s wanting to reach Broughton or Moss! *[Denbighshire Record Office]*

### 101. BRYMBO STATION, 1935

Brymbo station became surrounded by the steelworks and its slag tips once the passenger service was withdrawn in 1917, although in this 1935 view the station building still remained intact. *[Denbighshire Record Office]*

**102. BRYMBO, 1966**
After withdrawal of the short-lived passenger service, the expanding steelworks eventually obliterated the GC station. On 19 August BR Standard Class 4 4-6-0 75033 hauls a train of steel bars past the site of Brymbo Station. *[J. M. Tolson]*

# The Wrexham & Minera Joint Railway – Brymbo to Coed Talon

**103. GLASCOED VIADUCT, 1919**
Between Brymbo and Coed Talon there were two major engineering features; Glascoed VIaduct and Ffrith Viaduct. The former is illustrated here. Despite the rural appearance of the landscape this was a significant mining and quarrying district up until the 1960s. *[John Ryan Collection]*

**104. LLANFYNYDD** *c.*1920

Station staff and train crew pose in front of a LNWR 'Coal Tank' locomotive with a short freight train for Brymbo. Llanfynydd station consisted of a single wooden platform with wooden buildings providing a general office, waiting room, ladies waiting room and lavatories. *[J. Dixon Collection]*

**105. COED TALON, 1963**
Long after the end of passenger services rail enthusiasts swarm around the station and surrounding area after the arrival of a DMU charter train. *[J. Ryan]*

# Lines in the Moss Valley

### Introduction

In the 19th Century the Moss Valley was an industrialised area extending from Gatewen Colliery in the south to Ffrwd Ironworks in the north. Five lines served the Moss Valley during its industrial heyday; the Brymbo & Minera, Brynmally and Ffrwd Branches of the North Wales Mineral Railway, the WM&CQ Ffrwd Branch and the GWR Moss Valley Branch.

### North Wales Mineral Railway, Brymbo & Minera Branch

The NWM Brymbo & Minera Branch was the first railway to enter the Moss Valley. While the section between Brymbo and Minera was a conventional branch line as described elsewhere in this book, the section between Wheatsheaf Junction, north of Wrexham on the Shrewsbury & Chester main line, to Brymbo via Moss included two rope-worked inclines and two tunnels. It was opened in July 1847 but with the opening of the Croes

Newydd to Broughton line in May 1862 it became redundant as the access from the S&C to Brymbo and so the incline between Moss and Brymbo was closed. The lower incline between Moss and Gwersyllt was closed in October 1908 and the remaining section between Gwersyllt and Wheatsheaf Junction was closed in 1951.

### North Wales Mineral Railway, Brynmally & Ffrwd Branches

Following the opening of the NWM Brymbo & Minera Branch, a number of smaller feeder branches were built. Two of these, opened in November 1847, extended northwards from Moss to Brynmally colliery and the collieries & ironworks at Ffrwd. The Brynmally branch survived until 1935 while the Ffrwd branch was cut back to Westminster Colliery in 1917 following the closure of Ffrwd Ironworks in 1905 and closed completely in 1925.

### WM&CQ Railway, Ffrwd Branch

In order to take a share in the prosperity of the industry of the Ffrwd area, the WM&CQ opened a branch from Ffrwd Junction, between Gwersyllt and Cefn-y-bedd on its main line, to Ffrwd ironworks and the collieries of the area. This branch was in use between 1866 and 1935.

### GWR, Moss Valley Branch

This line, opened on 11 May 1882 between Moss Valley Junction and Moss,

As well as being the terminus for the passenger service from Wrexham, Moss Halt was also the junction for Brynmally and Westminster Collieries, as shown in the plan. Moss Sidings Signal Box was only opened when access to the sidings was required. The frame was unlocked by a key on the electric train staff for the Moss Valley Junction to Moss section and was worked by the Moss signalman. The electric train staff instrument for the section was housed in the station building at Moss Halt. A 'one engine in steam' train staff was used between Moss Halt and Brynmally Colliery.

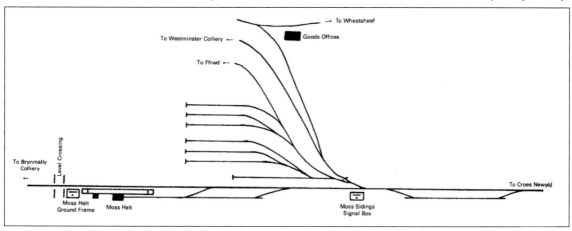

was intended to improve access to Moss in the same way as the Croes Newydd to Broughton line of 1862 had improved access to Brymbo. Unlike all the other branches in the Moss Valley which were for freight traffic only, this line had a passenger service between May 1905 and December 1930. The GWR railmotor service served halts at Gatewen, Pentre Broughton, Gwersyllt Hill and Moss. After withdrawal of the passenger service with effect from 1st January 1931 the line reverted to freight-only status until complete closure in 1935 following the closure of Brynmally Colliery. A short section of the branch was reopened in the 1960s to serve a disposal point for opencast coal at Gatewen but this has now been closed and lifted.

**106. VRON BRANCH, 1959**
A rare view of the single line junction from the Vron Colliery on the GC line. The left hand branch is to Brymbo Works and the GWR whilst the right hand branch is their line back to Brymbo station. *[R. W. Miller]*

**107. MOSS HALT, *c*.1910**

The terminus for the passenger service from Wrexham to Moss, which operated between 1 May 1905 and 31 December 1930, was known by a number of names during its short existence. GWR working timetables described it as Moss Halt; in this photograph the nameboard reads Moss Crossing Halt and other Authors' have variously referred to it as Moss Platform or Moss Station. *[L&GRP Collection]*

**108. GATEWEN, 1965**

A short section of the GWR Moss Valley Branch, from Moss Valley Junction to Gatewen, was reopened in the 1960s to serve the National Coal Board Opencast Executive's Gatewen Disposal Point which had previously been served from Brymbo North Junction on the WM&CQ main line. Between 1957 and 1966 the Robert Stephenson & Hawthorns built 0-6-0ST pictured here, 7162 of 1944, was used at Gatewen. Although originally built to dispatch local opencast coal, the Gatewen site was also used to stockpile coal mined at other collieries and during the summer of 1983 many thousands of tons were brought in by rail from Point of Ayr Colliery near Prestatyn. This traffic ceased in August 1983 when a derailment damaged track at Gatewen and the line then lay out of use for six years until it was lifted at the end of 1989. *[P. G. Hindley]*

**109. GATEWEN, 1979**
During the 1970s the firm of Lindley Plant Ltd were operating the site on behalf of the NCB. They used ex-BR Class 03 0-6-0
D2182 seen here shunting loaded wagons in July 1979. *[Trefor Thompson]*

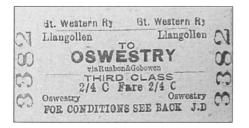

# The Wrexham, Mold & Connah's Quay Railway

The lines making up the Wrexham, Mold & Connah's Quay Railway (WM&CQ) system were built in stages over a thirty year period between 1860 and 1890. The Buckley Railway was promoted by local businessmen to link the brickworks and collieries of Buckley with the port of Connah's Quay on the River Dee. The steeply-graded single line, which closely followed the course of an earlier tramway, was opened in 1862. The first section of the WM&CQ was opened in 1866 between Wrexham; where there was a junction with the Great Western Railway, and Buckley; where there was a junction with the Buckley Railway and hence a link with Connah's Quay. The WM&CQ and Buckley companies worked closely together and in 1873 the WM&CQ took over the Buckley Railway on a 999 year lease.

The 1880s were a decade of expansion for the WM&CQ during which four major projects were undertaken. In 1887 a new section of line was opened between Wrexham Exchange and Wrexham Central, so bringing the WM&CQ into the heart of its home town. The section of the existing main line between Wrexham Exchange and Buckley Junction was doubled in 1888, the line having originally been built as a single line on a double track formation. Probably the most important project was the line known as the 'Hawarden Loop'; a double track line between Buckley Junction and Connah's Quay & Shotton where an end-on junction was made with the Manchester, Sheffield & Lincolnshire Railway's (MS&L) westward link from Chester via the Hawarden Bridge. This link with the MS&L, opened on 31 March 1890, marked the beginning of the end of the WM&CQ's independent existence.

During the 1890s the poor state of the WM&CQ's financial health saw it move closer to the MS&L, with whom it was jointly engaged in promoting the construction of a line northwards from Hawarden Bridge through the Wirral to Bidston. A court case in 1897 saw the WM&CQ pass into receivership and effectively into the control of the MS&L's successor, the Great Central Railway. In 1905 both the WM&CQ and the Buckley Railway were officially absorbed by the Great Central which in turn became part of the London & North Eastern Railway on the grouping of Britain's railways in 1923.

The decline of the brick making industry in the Buckley area lead to the closure of the Buckley Railway in two stages, from Connah's Quay to Northop Hall in 1959 and from Northop Hall to Buckley Junction in 1965. Apart from Hope Exchange, which closed in 1958, all the passenger stations on the WM&CQ remain open although all except Shotton are unstaffed. Today there is an hourly service from Wrexham Central to Bidston while the main freight traffic on the line is steel coil between the Corus plants at Llanwern and Shotton.

*Facing page:* **110. WREXHAM, 1948**
Taken by an RAF photo-reconnaissance training flight on 17 November 1948, this view looking north gives shows all three of Wrexham's stations and much of the town's other railway infrastructure. Particularly prominent in the centre of the picture is the large goods shed at Wrexham Central. As a reminder that Britain's railways had been nationalised for less than a year at the time this photograph was taken, on the original print "British Railways" can be seen on the tender of the locomotive, possibly an ex-LNER J39 0-6-0, shunting coal wagons at the west end of Wrexham Central station platforms. In contrast with the earlier view (below) the Cambrian Railways loco shed and turntable have now been removed. Towards the upper left edge of the picture Wrexham General and Wrexham Exchange are partly obscured by smoke from the Wrexham Lager Brewery although at least two locomotives can be seen on the Great Western line; one under the Mold Road bridge and another close to Wrexham North signal box. *[National Assembly for Wales]*

*Below:* **111. WREXHAM, c.1910**
A fine early 20th century view looking east over Bradley Road bridge towards Wrexham Central. The double track WMCQ main line ran between the line of wagons and line of carriages in the left foreground. Note that the carriage sidings extend under the bridge and and right up to Wrexham Central signal box. Beyond the bridge the large goods shed and extensive sidings may be seen to the north of the line while on the south side are the Cambrian Railways' loco shed and turntable. *[W. Alister Williams Collection]*

**112. WREXHAM, *c*.1980**
This view looking west emphasises the tight curvature of the singled WM&CQ main line as it descends from Wrexham Exchange (just visible at the extreme right hand edge of the picture) into the town centre at Wrexham Central (off picture bottom right). At the time this picture was taken there was still healthy parcels and postal traffic from Wrexham General, as evidenced by the vans in the bay platforms at the south end of the station. *[W. Alister Williams Collection]*

**113. WREXHAM, 1887**
A view during the early stages of construction of Wrexham Central station following the decision to extend the WM&CQ line from its previous terminus at the Exchange station. The workmen appear to have a captive audience of well dressed ladies and gentlemen. St Mark's church is in the background.
*[W. Alister Williams Collection]*

**114. WREXHAM, 1966**
At one time Wrexham Central could boast four platforms, two signal boxes and an extensive goods yard. The decline had already started when this view was taken, as illustrated by the removal of the sidings into and behind the goods shed, 30 May 1966. *[H. B. Priestley - Pacer Archives Collection]*

**115. WREXHAM, 1939**

In this view looking westwards a train from Seacombe headed by LNER Class C13 4-4-2T 5456 has arrived in one of the through platforms which were also used by Great Western trains on the Ellesmere line.   *[C. A. Appleton]*

**116. WREXHAM, *c*.1955**

An animated scene at Central station as a Saturday morning 'Rattler' from Seacombe headed by BR Standard 2-6-2T 82000 arrives and disgorges its passengers.

*[W. Alister Williams Collection]*

**117. WREXHAM, *c*.1966**

In 1961 the dieselisation of rural railways reached Wrexham, as depicted by the Derby built DMU sets which replaced steam trains on the services to Chester and the Wirral, where New Brighton replaced Seacombe as their terminus. The sets were normally made up of two power cars to cope with the inclines between Shotton and Buckley Junction.

*[H. B. Priestley - Pacer Archives Collection]*

**118. WREXHAM, *c*.1950**
Wrexham Exchange station in early BR days was little changed from pre-grouping days with its distinctive platform lamps. Note the plethora of poster boards, probably advertising holiday resorts for which the railway was still the main form of transport. *[W. Alister Williams Collection]*

**119. WREXHAM, *c*.1980**
An interior view of Wrexham Exchange Signal Box showing several old style telephones, the train register and a pot belly stove. Also visible are the signalman's friends - his armchair and his kettle. *[A. Cliff]*

**120. WREXHAM, 2005**

At the time this photograph was taken the surviving Wrexham to Bidston passenger service was usually provided by a single Class 153 unit, as seen here arriving at Platform 4 of Wrexham General, previously Wrexham Exchange. Additional funding for the service from the Welsh Assembly Government has subsequently enabled Arriva Trains Wales to introduce two car Class 150 units. The line is supported by an active users' group and is marketed as the 'Borderlands' line. The possibility of electrification and integration of the service into the Merseyrail network is periodically suggested. *[George Jones]*

**121. WREXHAM, 2005**

A Network Rail test train 'topped & tailed' by Class 37 locomotives owned by freight operator DRS is seen at Wrexham General after traversing the line from Bidston. *[George Jones]*

**122. WREXHAM, 1969**

A view from the platform end of Exchange station looking towards Exchange signal box, on the left, from which a complicated arrangement of junction lines with slip points gave access to all the former GWR lines served by Wrexham North signal box, on the right. This involved complex interlocking and special instructions to the signalmen when trains were exchanged. The layout was drastically simplified as part of an overall rationalisation in the mid 1980s. Note the GWR lower quadrant bracket signals contrasting with the upper quadrant signal on the former LNER line.

*[H. B. Priestley - Pacer Archives Collection]*

**123. WREXHAM,** *c.1939*

Rhosddu shed in LNER days, viewed looking north across the running lines. On shed are examples of two classes of locomotive associated with the Wrexham area in the first half of the 20th century. On the left is a J10 0-6-0 tender engine for working goods trains while on the right is a 4-4-2 tank engine of the C13 Class which were the mainstay of passenger services to Seacombe and Chester Northgate throughout GCR and LNER ownership of the line.

*[B. Roberts – J. Peden Collection]*

**124. WREXHAM, 1970**
Brymbo North Signal Box controlled the northern access from the WM&CQ main line to the WM&CQ branch to Brymbo. *[M. A. King]*

**125. GWERSYLLT, *c*.1905**
An overall view at Gwersyllt showing the original passenger station and goods yard as depicted in a sepia postcard of the period.
*[W. Alister Williams Collection]*

**126. CAERGWRLE, *c*.1905**

Earlier in the last century Caergwrle Castle was a popular destination for excursion passengers from Seacombe and in the 1930s the LNER produced a booklet entitled *Rambles Around Caergwrle* in order to encourage the use of walking tour tickets by Merseysiders. The standard wooden signal box, supplied by the Railway Signal Company, and yellow brick waiting shelter can be clearly seen in this Edwardian view. *[Heyday Publishing Company]*

**127. PENYFFORDD, *c*.1965**

An overall view of Penyffordd showing the station buildings before demolition and the signal box, which was later replaced by a BR standard structure. *[Lens of Sutton]*

**128. PENYFFORDD, *c.*1967**

An enthusiasts' special train, 'The WM&CQ Railtour' rejoins its 'own' line via the spur after visiting Rhydymwyn, which by this time was the extremity of the former LNWR line from Mold Junction to Denbigh. The signal box at the platform end had by now been renamed by BR, having been 'Hope Junction' until the 1950s. The station was also known as Hope Junction until August 1877 when it became Penyffordd for Leeswood. [*J. Barlow*]

**129. PENYFFORDD, *c.*1995**

Changing times at Penyffordd. The signal box has now been replaced with a standard BR Type 15 structure and the train is a Class 142 'Pacer' unit, developed at government behest in the 1980s for rural services and based on a bus body design.
*[Dave Southern]*

**130. HOPE EXCHANGE, *c.*1955**

While freight transfers between the former LNER and LMS lines were exchanged via the curve at Penyffordd, passengers made use of Hope Exchange, an isolated station with no road access at the point where the two lines crossed. The station closed in 1958 leaving any passengers who wished to transfer between the two routes having to walk from Penyffordd (GC) and Hope & Penyffordd (LNWR), as the nearest two stations were distinguished, or vice versa. *[Flintshire Record Office]*

**131. PADESWOOD, 1988**
No.6, works number 10235 of 1965, was one of a pair of Sentinel diesel locomotives which worked at Castle Cement's Padeswood works from 1976 to 1991. Both were transferred to Padeswood from another of the company's plants at West Thurrock in Essex. *[Dave Southern]*

**132. PADESWOOD, 1988**
The weighbridge provided a convenient location for stabling Padeswood works' active locomotives at weekends. Prior to arrival in North Wales this Yorkshire Engine Company 0-4-0 diesel locomotive pictured here worked at the company's Pitstone works alongside the West Coast Main Line in Buckinghamshire. After rail traffic ceased at Padeswood in 1991 it moved to Llangollen for preservation. In contrast to the experience at many other previously rail-served industrial sites, inbound rail traffic subsequently resumed in the form of a regular flow of coal from Healey Mills near Wakefield. *[Dave Southern]*

**133. BUCKLEY JUNCTION, 1969**
The distinctive station buildings provided here were constructed from locally produced monochromed yellow bricks with stone lintels and redbrick quoins and dentils. *[V. J .Bradley]*

**134. BUCKLEY JUNCTION, 1934**
LNER Class N5 0-6-2T 5922, one of a class of locomotive associated with the line for over 50 years, standing 'wrong line' at Buckley Junction during shunting operations. The first examples appeared in 1896 and were built by Beyer Peacock for the WM&CQ as their Nos. 17 & 18. The GCR, which absorbed the WM&CQ in 1905, adopted them as a standard type and several worked on the neighbouring Cheshire Lines Railway. The 'flowerpot' chimneys were added by the LNER.
*[R .E. Thomas]*

**135. BUCKLEY JUNCTION, *c*.1968**
In a practice virtually unchanged for one hundred years, but which has now been almost entirely eradicated from Britain's railways, a BR Class 24 diesel locomotive on a local trip working from Croes Newydd yard shunts the goods yard at Buckley Junction on a Winter's day. The wagons and brake van are stood on the last remaining section of the original WM&CQ line to Buckley, while to the right is what the WM&CQ referred to as their 'Hawarden Loop', the line via Shotton and the Hawarden Bridge over the River Dee which retains regular passenger and freight services today. *[J. Thomas]*

**136. BUCKLEY OLD, 1934**
Buckley Old, as the former terminus of the WM&CQ in Buckley became known following the opening of Buckley Junction station on the Hawarden Loop, finally closed to passengers in 1895 but remained open for freight until 1965. The locomotive at the head of a short freight heading for the junction is LNER J60 0-6-0T 6408 which was originally built by Kitson of Leeds in 1895 for the Lancashire, Derbyshire & East Coast Railway. When, like the WM&CQ, the LD&EC became part of the Great Central Railway the GCR authorities identified this class of locomotive as being particularly suitable for use on its industrial branches in the Wrexham area. *[R. E. Thomas]*

**137. ASHTON'S BRANCH, 1934**

The line to Buckley served numerous brickworks along its route. In this view the LNER J60 0-6-0T 6408 and crew pose with an elderly gentleman, possibly an ex-railwayman, near a level crossing on this branch. *[R .E. Thomas]*

**138. HAWARDEN, *c*.1905**

An overall view of Hawarden, W. E. Gladstone's local station, looking towards Shotton. *[Lens of Sutton]*

**139. HAWARDEN, 1968**

Taken from a train departing Hawarden for Wrexham, this picture shows the signal box provided by the GCR together with the substantial goods shed. *[H. B. Priestley - Pacer Archives Collection]*

**140. HAWARDEN BRIDGE, 1968**

A driver's eye view of the principal engineering feature of the line opened on 3 August 1889, the first and largest span of which was a swing bridge over the canalised section of the River Dee. The swing bridge was immobilised in the 1960s and the tall and distinctive control tower was later demolished. *[H. B. Priestley - Pacer Archives Collection]*

**141. DEE MARSH JUNCTION, 1968**

Once across the bridge the line passes into England. Here at Dee Marsh signal box the route is set for the Chester line, which closed to passengers in 1968. In the 1966/7 timetable there were twenty-seven weekday services in each direction between Shotton High level and Chester Northgate with a typical journey time of fourteen minutes.  *[H. B. Priestley - Pacer Archives Collection]*

# Ruabon, Rhos, Acrefair & Llangollen

## Introduction

The area to the south west of Wrexham, around the towns of Rhosllanercherog, Ruabon and Acrefair, was an important industrial district from the late 18th to mid 20th centuries, with coal mining, brick making, chemical manufacture and various metal trades all represented. The area was initially served by a series of local tramways, which over time were supplemented by and combined with a series of branches from the Shrewsbury & Chester main line. The opening of the Vale of Llangollen Railway's line from Ruabon to Llangollen, the first stage of a through route to Barmouth on the Cardigan Bay coast, further improved access to the area with connections made at Trevor.

## The Pontcysyllte Branch

The Llangollen Canal, or the Ellesmere Canal as it was known at the time of construction, was opened to the basin at the north end of Thomas Telford's spectacular Pontcysyllte Aqueduct in 1805. In order to provide a regular supply of coal traffic to the new canal, a horse-worked double track tramway was built to link several collieries in Acrefair with the canal basin. One interesting feature of the tramway as first built was the crane part way along its route which was used to transfer wagons between levels. As part of the Aqueduct opening ceremony on 21 November 1805 five wagonloads of local coal were drawn by horses to the basin and loaded into two of the boats in the ceremonial procession.

The tramway was later extended, first to Plas Madoc Colliery in 1808 and then a year later to Wynn Hall Colliery and Afon Eitha Colliery south of Rhos. In 1846 the Ellesmere Canal Company became part of the Shropshire Union Railways and Canal Company which in turn was leased by the London and North Western Railway Company (LNWR), giving that company access to an area that was a Great Western Railway (GWR) stronghold.

With the coming of the Vale of Llangollen Railway the LNWR decided to convert the tramway into a locomotive worked single track standard gauge railway and to extend it to Llwyneinion Brickworks north of Rhos. The conversion was carried out in stages and the line reopened fully in January 1867. The first locomotive to work the line was provided by one of the local industries, the New British Iron Company. However, in December 1870 an 0-4-0 tank locomotive arrived from the LNWR works at Crewe and worked the branch until it returned to Crewe for scrapping in March 1883.

The decline of the line began in the 1870s when a number of the small collieries in the area closed. In 1882 the Wynne Hall Spelter Works closed while in 1886 closure of the line's most important customer, the New British Ironworks, took place. Traffic from Wynnstay Colliery and Delph Brickworks was passed to the GWR via the Plas Madoc branch.

In 1896 the LNWR sold the line, except for the canal basin itself, to the GWR for £51,000. By the terms of the purchase the GWR was empowered to convert the line to carry passenger traffic. In 1901 the former tramway, by then known as the Pontcysyllte branch, joined up with the south end of the newly-opened GWR Rhos branch. The decline of industries in the area and the ability of the remaining industries to route their traffic onto the GWR system via Trevor, Rhos or the Plas Madoc branch meant that the canal basin fell into disuse as a freight transfer point. However, the basin remained in use as a watering point for the locomotive which worked the branch and the GWR Chester Division Report of 1925 stated that 'a small GWR boiler for pumping water into the tank has been fixed in the old warehouse which at one time served as a transfer warehouse and also as an engine shed for the Shropshire Union Canal Company'. For the remainder of its life following the GWR takeover the Pontcysyllte branch was served from Trevor via J. C. Edwards' private line, as described below. GWR freight trains regularly served Acrefair low level goods yard, Messrs. Hughes & Lancaster's engineering works on the site of the old New British Ironworks, Wynn Hall siding and Pant Brickworks. In 1953 the section between Pant and Hughes & Lancaster's works was closed.

**The Rhos Branch**

The 3³/₄ mile long Rhos Branch was built by the GWR in 1901. It left the Shrewsbury & Chester line a mile south of Wrexham General at Rhos Junction and although it was largely rural in nature its main purpose was to serve two brick works and three station goods yards.

Passenger services to Rhos with intermediate stations at Rhostyllen and Legacy commenced in 1901. In 1905 steam railmotors were introduced and the passenger service was extended to Wynn Hall Halt on the Pontcysyllte Branch south of Rhos and Ponkey Crossing Halt on the Ponkey Branch south of Legacy. The passenger service was subject to competition from the local omnibus operators and trams which operated between Wrexham and Johnstown. The services between Rhos and Wynn Hall Halt and Legacy and Ponkey Crossing Halt ceased on 22 March 1915 while the Rhos service lasted until 1 January 1931. However, a service was provided for the Welsh National Eisteddfod which was held at Rhos in 1945 and regular football excursions to Wrexham's home matches continued until the 1950s. Residual freight traffic finally ceased on 14 October 1963.

### The Plas Madoc Branch

The Plas Madoc branch was first opened in 1829 as a tramway similar to the Pontcysyllte branch. Its original purpose was to link Wynnstay Colliery with the New British Ironworks and to serve the Delph Brickworks. Its fortunes closely followed those of the Pontcysyllte branch; conversion to a single track railway partly on a new route took place in 1867 and the line was worked by the New British Ironworks until their liquidation in 1886. The Wynnstay Colliery Company then took over the working of the line, an arrangement which continued even after the GWR bought the line in 1896. Closure of the line as a link to the GWR main line at Ruabon took place in 1927 following the closure of Wynnstay Colliery. The section between Plas Madoc and Delph remained in use until 1953 for trains from the Rhos direction which ran to Plas Madoc sidings to reverse before proceeding to the brickworks at Delph.

### J. C. Edwards' Private Line

The line from Trevor station on the Ruabon to Llangollen line to the Pontcysyllte branch is of particular interest as it was originally built as a private siding. Following the opening of the Vale of Llangollen Railway in 1862, J. C. Edwards built a quarter mile long line in order to link their brickworks at Trefynant with the main line at Trevor. The Pontcysyllte branch was linked to Edwards' line in 1864 and soon afterwards the GWR and the LNWR negotiated running powers over it, paying Edwards one penny per ton of goods conveyed.

The conversion of the original Pontcysyllte tramway to standard gauge, the GWR purchase of the Pontcysyllte branch in 1896 and the decline in use of the canal basin all contributed to the increased importance of this section of line.

The GWR grouped Trevor to Rhos as one branch, operating it from both ends with traffic to and from stations north of Wrexham routed via Rhos and traffic to and from stations south of Ruabon routed via Trevor.

When the Pontcysyllte branch was cut back in 1953 this line was unaffected and continued to serve Edwards' brickworks and the large Monsanto Chemical Works built on the site of the much earlier Plas Kynaston Chemical Works and Ironworks. The brickworks closed in 1964 and the line finally closed on 1 January 1968 when rail traffic to Monsanto ceased.

## The Ponkey Branch

The Ponkey Branch was opened as a 1³/₄ mile long siding off the GWR main line from Gardden Lodge Junction just north of Ruabon station to furnaces at Ponkey and Aberderfyn on 1 August 1868. On 27 August 1876 the line was extended a further 1¹/₄ miles to Legacy. When the Rhos Branch was built the Ponkey Branch was connected to it at Legacy and on 5 June 1905 a steam railmotor service was introduced on the branch serving Fennant Road Halt, Aberderfyn Halt and Ponkey Crossing Halt. The passenger service was withdrawn on 22 March 1915 and two years later the branch was severed south of Legacy. The south end remained open to serve two brickworks, a petroleum siding, a furniture factory and a gas works. The branch, which was operated using a one engine in steam train staff kept in Ruabon North Signal Box, finally closed on 31 August 1964.

## Roberts & Maginnis Private Siding

This line ran from the north side of the Vale of Llangollen line at Trevor, across the A539 Ruabon to Llangollen road on the level and into Roberts and Maginnis Trevor Brickworks. Over the years the works was home to three industrial locomotives. The first was a Manning Wardle 0-4-0 saddle tank named *F. W. Cooper* which was replaced in 1937 by *Coronation*, an 0-4-0 saddle tank built by Peckett of Bristol as works number 1255 in 1911. Dieselisation came in 1951 when an 0-4-0 diesel mechanical locomotive was delivered new from John Fowler & Company of Leeds. Rail traffic ceased in 1966 and the diesel was sold to Crump's Wagon Works at Connah's Quay the following year.

## The Vale of Llangollen Railway

As already noted, the Vale of Llangollen Railway opened to freight at the end of 1861 and to passengers in mid 1862 as the first stage of what became a through route to Corwen, Bala, Dolgellau and Barmouth completed in 1869. Initially built as a single line, the section between Llangollen Line Junction at Ruabon and Llangollen Goods Junction, half a mile west of Llangollen station, was doubled in 1900. Llangollen was a popular destination for excursion traffic and from the late 1940s to the early 1960s considerable effort was made to encourage visitors to travel to the annual International Eisteddfod by train. Dr Beeching's 'Reshaping of British Railways' report decreed that all traffic to and from the Cambrian Coast should travel via Shrewsbury and so the withdrawal of services between Ruabon to Barmouth line was scheduled for January 1965. However, as a result of flood damage along the Dee Valley in December 1964, Llangollen became a terminus for the final month and passengers were conveyed forward to Bala by bus from where they resumed their journey to the coast by train. A residual freight service from Ruabon to Llangollen, calling at Trevor en route, was retained until April 1968. Demolition began soon afterwards but in the early 1970s the preservationists of the Flint & Deeside Railway Preservation Society identified Llangollen as a suitable base for their ambitions to develop a standard gauge heritage railway in North Wales. Initial push-pull operations from Llangollen station to a point close to Llangollen Goods Junction began in July 1981 and have subsequently been extended westwards in stages as far as the present terminus at Carrog. Corwen remains the ultimate goal, but in the other direction back towards Ruabon a number of developments have encroached upon the trackbed making restoration unlikely.

**142. TREVOR, *c*.1900**
A speciality of the late Victorian and early Edwardian eras was the posed station photograph when all the staff together with their families, not forgetting the dog, turned out in their 'Sunday best' for the photographer. To complete the picture the loco department have also turned out a well groomed GWR 0-4-2T 'Metro' tank with open cab. *[Authors' Collection]*

**143. LLANGOLLEN, 1962**

A wintry scene at Llangollen as a train for Corwen and Bala awaits departure. *[H. J. Leadbetter]*

**144. LLANGOLLEN, c.1966**

After withdrawal of passenger services in 1965 a daily freight trip continued to operate to Llangollen goods yard for three more years. In this view the photographer is looking west with Llangollen Goods Junction signal box visible in the distance and the line to the goods yard, which is behind the photographer, is on the right. A GWR 0-6-0PT departs for Ruabon with a short train of empty mineral wagons. Although the track layout is slightly different, the scene is very similar today with a new signal box having been constructed on the site by Llangollen Railway volunteers in the late 1980s. *[J. Hillman]*

**145. LLANGOLLEN, 1993**

The Preservation Era. A BR Standard Class 4 2-6-4T takes water at Llangollen's Platform 2. The locomotive is actually 80079 from the Severn Valley Railway but during the visit it was disguised as classmate 80072 which was undergoing restoration at Llangollen at the time. *[A. O. Wynn]*

PRIVATE.—For Company's Servants only.

# GREAT WESTERN RAILWAY.

Circular No. R. 1176.
T.S. 26667.

Chief Goods Manager's Office,
Paddington Station, London, W.,
*September 28th,* 1901.

## OPENING OF WREXHAM AND RHOS LINE.

This Line will be opened for General Merchandize and Mineral Traffic on 1st October.

The Stations and Sidings thereon are :—

| Station or Siding. | Distance from Wrexham Station. | Distance from Ruabon Station. | Distance from Trevor Station. |
|---|---|---|---|
| | miles. | miles. | miles. |
| Rhostyllen ... ... ... | 1¼ | 4½ | 6½ |
| Legacy ... ... ... ... | 3 | 3½ | 5½ |
| Rhos (near Ruabon) ... ... | 4½ | 4 | 4 |
| Wynn Hall Siding ... ... | 5½ | 5½ | 2½ |

The undermentioned accommodation is provided :—

**Rhostyllen** ... Goods Warehouse and Sidings.
At present there is no Crane, Weighbridge, Cattle Pen, nor Carriage Shoot.
The Company will not undertake Cartage, and rates must not be quoted as including that service.

**Legacy** ... ... Only Station to Station Traffic not requiring covering will be dealt with at this place.
There is no Warehouse, Crane or Weighbridge.
Traffic must be invoiced to **"Rhos for Legacy."**

**Rhos** (near Ruabon) Goods Warehouse, Sidings, Cart Weighbridge, and Crane capable of lifting 30 cwts.
At present there is no Cattle Pen nor Carriage Shoot.
A Cartage Staff will be provided.
Traffic for the undermentioned Works to be invoiced from or to Rhos :—
Pant Brick Works.
Copy        ,,        ,,
Llwynenion ,,        ,,

**Wynn Hall Siding** Only Station to Station Traffic not requiring covering will be dealt with at this place.
There is no Warehouse, Crane or Weighbridge.
Traffic must be invoiced to **"Rhos for Wynn Hall Siding."**

Traffic between your Station and Rhostyllen, Legacy, Rhos and Wynn Hall Siding must be treated as local and abstracted accordingly.

If you require any rates for Traffic to or from these places application can be made for them to your District Goods Manager, to whom please forward acknowledgment of this Circular.

**L. W. MAIDEN.**

**146. NOTICE OF OPENING – RHOS LINE**
*[Authors' Collection]*

**147. RHOSTYLLEN,** *c.*1905
An early view of Rhostyllen station probably taken soon after opening in 1905. The neat and tidy appearance shows how the staff of the period took a pride in their station. *[Welsh Industrial and Maritime Museum – GWR Archive Collection]*

**148. RHOS, *c*.1905**
Another early view taken at Rhos station soon after opening in 1905.
*[Welsh Industrial and Maritime Museum – GWR Archive Collection]*

**149. RHOS, 1957**
GWR 0-6-0PT 1635 on the 1pm Croes Newydd South Fork to Pant freight at Rhos station. *[H. Davies]*

**150. RHOS, 1959**

An enthusiasts' special arrives at the now disused platform and overgrown tracks behind two GWR 0-6-0PTs, 1660 and 1635, on 18 September 1959. *[A. Donaldson]*

**151. RHOS, 1959**

Another view on the same day as the locomotives run round their special train.  *[H. C. Casserley]*

**152. RHOS, 1957**
A typical level crossing between Rhos and Pant at Brook Street. *[H. Davies]*

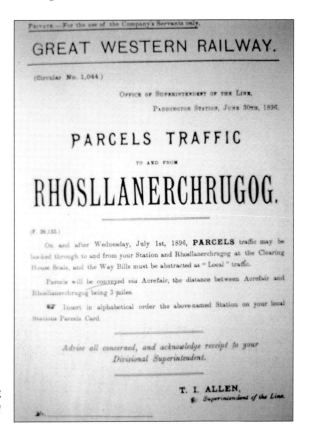

**153. PARCELS TRAFFIC NOTICE**
*[Authors' Collection]*

**154. TREVOR, 1948**
A well groomed Peckett 0-4-0ST, works number 1255 of 1911, seen at Trevor Silica Works on 28 July 1948.
*[Kidderminster Railway Museum]*

**155. HUGHES & LANCASTER, 1957**
GWR 0-6-0PT 1659 shunting at Hughes & Lancaster's Siding prior to working the 3.55pm freight to Trevor on 16 August
1957. *[H. Davies]*

**156. J. C. EDWARDS, 1957**
GWR 0-6-0PT 1659 shunting J. C. Edwards' Trevor
Brickworks on 16 August 1957. [*H. Davies*]

**157. PLAS MADOC, 1974**
A rare view of the overgrown track bed of the former Plas
Madoc branch looking towards Wynnstay Colliery and the
junction with the main line at Ruabon South. The over
bridge carries the main A539 Llangollen – Ruabon road.
Beyond the bridge there was originally a level crossing
over the road from Penycae. [*R. W. Miller*]

### 158. FRONCYSYLLTE, 1954

Pen-y-craig quarry at Froncysyllte was a limestone quarry high above the Ellesmere and Llangollen canal. A tramway descended by incline to the first level where there was a side quarry and horses took over to transport the wagons to the top of a second incline and then down to a third incline. At one time there were two branches, one in a tunnel under the A5 road and the other across the A5 road to limekilns with their tops at road level. Up until 1954 one could see two men with red flags holding up the road traffic for the horse and wagons to cross. After the limekilns closed the wagons, which were of the side tipping type, crossed the road and went on to a loading platform for tipping into a crushing plant where the stone was coated with tar ready for road construction. In this view there is no sign of flagmen as the horseman hurries his charge across the A5 with two loaded wagons. *[John Thomas Collection]*

### 159. FRONCYSYLLTE, 1954

A view looking towards the quarry, which is above the tree line, with wagons coming down the incline. These will be hitched to the waiting horse to be hauled across the A5 road. Note also the weighbridge hut and bench. *[John Thomas Collection]*

# Wrexham & Ellesmere Railway

It seems inconceivable today that the sleepy town of Ellesmere in Shropshire once figured in a 'battle' as a staging post in the struggles of various promoters to build railways from England into Wales or vice versa.

The independent promoters of a railway to link the Oswestry & Newtown line with the LNWR at Whitchurch were understandably opposed by the mighty GWR who offered to build a line from Rednal to Oswestry which would include a projected branch to Ellesmere. In Ellesmere the argument that the GWR scheme would bring the rural agricultural area into close touch with the North Wales coalfields was countered by the plea that the promoters of the independent company could also build a branch to Ruabon or Wrexham and powers to that effect "would be applied for as soon as what may be called the main line from Oswestry to Whitchurch was carried." From this statement the concept of a railway linking Ellesmere with Wrexham could perhaps be considered to have been spawned. However, although the Oswestry, Ellesmere & Whitchurch Railway obtained its Act of Parliament on 1 August 1861, the gestation period proved to be a long one.

Consistent with the moves to drive a railway eastwards from Oswestry, the WM&CQ promoted lines from Wrexham to Bettisfield in 1862 and from Wrexham to Whitchurch in 1864. These were more direct routes towards the important junction of Crewe and effectively by-passed Ellesmere. Both schemes were aborted and it was not until the WM&CQ came under the influence of the MS&L in the early 1880s that matters moved towards fruition. The MS&L's dynamic Chairman Sir Edward Watkin wished to unite with the Cambrian, who were at that time working the Mid-Wales Railway, with the idea of founding a Welsh Railways Union in order to provide an independent route between the collieries and ironworks of South Wales and Birkenhead.

Another scheme for a Wrexham to Bettisfield line was promoted in 1884 under the guise of the Denbighshire & Shropshire Junction Railway but it was the Wrexham & Ellesmere Railway, backed by the MS&L and incorporated by an Act of 31 July 1885, which despite numerous delays and extensions of time was begun in July 1892, completed in October 1895 and opened on 2 November 1895.

At Wrexham the line made an end-on junction with the WM&CQ which had extended its line to Wrexham Central in 1887 in early anticipation of the new line. The line was built with a double track formation but remained single throughout its life. The passing stations of Marchwiel, Bangor-on-Dee and Overton-on-Dee, in common with many others of the period, were sited some distance from the villages they served! The passing places were provided with delightful timber-built station buildings while the platform shelters had distinctive Gothic style arched openings which echoed the main building at Wrexham Central. This structure contrasted sharply with the "temporary" corrugated iron structures provided by the WM&CQ which survived beyond the end of passenger services on the Ellesmere line.

From the outset the new line was worked under agreement by the Cambrian who ordered no less than six 0-4-4T locomotives from Nasmyth Wilson & Company for use on the line. Three were delivered in time for the opening in 1895 with the remaining three following in 1899. At $45^{1}/_{2}$ tons they were some of the heaviest locomotives the Cambrian were to own. It appears, however, that more appropriate 2-4-0Ts were soon drafted in for passenger workings. A push-pull train made its debut in 1913 comprised of a 2-4-0T in combination with a bogie saloon built from two six-wheeled composite carriages.

It is recorded that in the early years there was a steady flow of freight traffic over the branch. In fact a $3^{1}/_{2}\%$ dividend was recorded for the last nine years of the Wrexham & Ellesmere's existence as an independent company - better than the Cambrian which did not pay a dividend at all in 1920 or 1921. How much of this lucrative trade can be attributed to the through traffic originally envisaged is not fully known.

The post-grouping GWR influence gradually resulted in a takeover by the more usual forms of GWR branch motive power such as 0-6-0PTs and the ubiquitous 0-4-2Ts although Dean and Collett 0-6-0s were also recorded on freight workings.

In addition to the three principal intermediate stations the motor-train concept was progressively exploited to the full by the introduction of Halts, the earliest of which go back to Cambrian days with Sesswick and Trench opened in 1913 and 1914 respectively. Further halts were introduced by the GWR during the 1930s and 1940s at Hightown (1932), Cloy (1932), Elson (1937) and Pickhill (1946), making a total of nine stops on a $12^{3}/_{4}$ mile journey.

The advent of the Second World War brought a whole new importance to this rural branch line. Connections to an extensive Royal Ordnance Factory combined with the line's strategic value as a diversionary yet direct route to the Wrexham coalfield and Merseyside resulted in the withdrawal of normal passenger services from 10 June 1940 until 6 May 1946, although workmen's trains did operate during this period. After the war a gradual decline in freight traffic set in and by 1950 services were down to two trips in each direction on weekdays. Passenger services, mainly push-pull 'Auto Trains', followed a consistent pattern throughout the life of the line with six trains each way initially subsequently increased to eight. After closure to passengers in September 1962 the line remained open for freight between Wrexham and Cadbury's private siding near Pickhill until 1973 when the line was cut back to Abenbury sidings, closure of this final section occurring in 1982.

Any description of the line would be incomplete without mention of the double track Ellesmere loop line which provided direct access from the branch to the Oswestry line and was part of Sir Edward Watkin's intended strategic route for through traffic between South & Mid Wales and the North West. The loop was authorised in 1895 and was built in the following year although it appears that it subsequently fell into disuse until the GCR developed seasonal through traffic to and from the Cardigan Bay resorts in the decade prior to the First World War.

**160. WREXHAM, 1959**
A typical branch line passenger service consisted of a GWR '14xx' Class 0-4-2T locomotive and a single Autocoach enabling the return working to be operated by the driver from a dedicated compartment at the rear of the coach, exemplified here by 1432 and coach ready to depart for Ellesmere. *[P. H. Groom]*

**161. WREXHAM, 1962**
Wrexham's distinctive Parish Church is prominent in this view of GWR '14xx' Class 0-4-2T 1458 leaving Wrexham Central with an auto-train working to Ellesmere on 25 August 1962  *[Brian Cowlishaw]*

**162. WREXHAM, 1914**
Men of the 4th Battalion
Royal Welsh Fusiliers
march into Central Station
en route to their annual
camp at Aberystwyth,
July 1914. The main
station building was a
former chapel, dismantled
and moved to Wrexham
from mid Wales. The
large sign on the right
reads: 'Cambrian
Railways Direct Service
To — London (Euston),
Birmingham (New Street),
South Wales,
Aberystwyth and the
Cardigan Bay Resorts ...'
*[W. Alister Williams
Collection]*

**163. WREXHAM, 1914**
With the large goods shed dominating the scene a packed troop train prepares to depart from Wrexham Central conveying
local Territorials to their annual camp at Aberystwyth in July 1914. A soldier with fixed bayonet patrols the trackside while a
number of military and civilian personnel look on. The loco partially visible on the left is a Great Central Railway Class 9F
(later LNER Class N5) 0-6-2T. *[W. Alister Williams Collection]*

**164. WREXHAM, 1905**

Cambrian Railways Nº7, a William Aston designed 0-4-4T built by Nasmyth, Wilson & Co of Manchester, was one of six such locomotives purchased specifically for use on the Wrexham–Ellesmere and Barmouth–Dolgellau branch lines for both freight and passenger trains. In this scene in Caia goods yard an employee from Meredith & Jones' Cambrian Leather Works stands alongside their dray and yard staff and the crew pose by their engine. *[H. Cudworth]*

**165. WREXHAM, *c*.1920**

A pre-1923 view of a typical Cambrian 4-4-0 locomotive built by Sharp, Stewart & Co. The loco crew and other staff in the uniforms of the period add character to the picture. In the left background is the Cambrian's loco shed while in the right background is the Great Central's very substantial brick-built goods shed.
*[Mike Grant via W. Alister Williams Collection]*

**166. HIGHTOWN, *c*.1962**
An animated scene at Hightown Halt in the days
when the train provided a 'suburban' service for the
local ladies' shopping trips to Wrexham.
*[Brian Cowlishaw]*

**167. HIGHTOWN, 1980**
In the final days of the branch a Class 25 diesel
propels empty china clay wagons past the site of
Hightown Halt in April 1980. The chimneys of the
brickworks at Abenbury can be seen in the distance.
*[Trefor Thompson]*

**168. ABENBURY VIADUCT, 1895**
An interesting view of the contractor's construction trains at work at Abenbury. The loco on the viaduct is probably the Manning Wardle 0-6-0ST *Weedon. [W. Alister Williams Collection]*

**169. ABENBURY VIADUCT, 1895**
Another view clearly illustrating how the ambitious railway promoters had the foresight to provide for possible future widening to double track, although in this case that never happened. *[W. Alister Williams Collection]*

## 170. ABENBURY BRICKWORKS, 1966

GWR 0-6-0PT 9610 shunts clay wagons at Abenbury Brickworks Siding during 1966. The section between Wrexham Central and Abenbury was the last part of the line to close, surviving until the early 1980s by which time Class 25 diesels had replaced Pannier Tanks on the Abenbury trip freight. *[Brian Taylor]*

## 171. MARCHWIEL, 1962

GWR '14xx' Class 0-4-2T 1417 enters Marchwiel with an Ellesmere train on 25 August 1962. Marchwiel was the first passing loop after leaving Wrexham. The station building here, and at the other two principal stations on the branch at Bangor-on-Dee and Overton-on Dee, was of substantial  timber construction providing all the essential facilities of a country station.

*[Brian Cowlishaw]*

**172. MARCHWIEL, 1964**
Driver Bob Humphries and Fireman Ivor Owen take a break at Marchwiel while working a trip freight to Cadbury's Siding in 1964. *[J. I. Owen]*

**173. PICKHILL HALT, 1962**
GWR '14xx' Class 0-4-2T 1458 arriving at Pickhill Halt with an Ellesmere train on 25 August 1962. This halt, which opened in 1946, had the basic wooden platform and a creosoted wooden shelter.  *[Brian Cowlishaw]*

**174. CADBURY'S SIDING, *c*.1965**
Beyond Sesswick Halt there was a private siding serving Cadbury's creamery. A GWR Pannier Tank is seen shunting the siding in the mid 1960s.   *[Brian Taylor]*

**175. BANGOR-ON-DEE, 1895**
Progress in construction techniques is demonstrated as manpower and horsepower are joined by the vertical boilered steam navvy.
*[Wrexham Leader]*

### 176. BANGOR-ON-DEE, *c.*1960
Located about one mile north east of Bangor-on-Dee, this single span lattice girder bridge carried the Wrexham–Ellesmere line over the Dee. It was one of the original structures, being built for the opening of the line in 1895 and remaining in use until closure in 1962. It was demolished in 1963. *[W. Alister Williams]*

### 177. BANGOR-ON-DEE, *c.*1962
A driver's eye view of the approach to the river bridge. *[Mike Lloyd / WRRC]*

**178. BANGOR-ON-DEE, 1962**

1458, a regular on the branch in the final months, arrives at Bangor-on-Dee with a train for Ellesmere on 7 September 1962. As the signalman exchanges the tokens a few passengers prepare to board the train. The lorry loaded with hay in the background gives a clue to the rural nature of the line. *[Brian Cowlishaw]*

**179. BANGOR-ON-DEE, 1962**

An auto-train for Wrexham is about to depart from Bangor-on-Dee. The signalman is walking back to his box with the token for the section from Overton in his left hand and a water can in the other. This photograph was taken on 7 September 1962, the day before closure. The weedy platform surface shows a distinct lack of use. The station lamps and the cast iron 'Beware of Trains' sign, an every day part of the station scene in 1962, are now regarded as prized collectors items.

*[Brian Cowlishaw]*

### 180. CLOY HALT, 1959
Cloy Halt was opened in July 1932 and consisted of a wooden edged ash filled platform with a standard GWR corrugated iron shelter. In this view 1432 is seen on an auto-train working on 9 April 1959. *[H. B. Priestley - Pacer Archives Collection]*

### 181. OVERTON-ON-DEE, 1963
The typical branch signal box seen here just after closure and with evidence of early dismantling on the platform. Cambrian boxes of this type were supplied by the signalling manufacturer Dutton of Worcester. *[H. J. Leadbetter]*

**182. OVERTON-ON-DEE, c.1955**

The rural nature of the Wrexham – Ellesmere line is apparent in this delightful view; the wooden buildings, Cambrian signal and the oil lamp on the bracket all combine to give a period atmosphere to the tranquil scene. The sidings are deserted and the lack of any goods or passenger traffic makes it obvious why the line closed. *[H. B. Priestley - Pacer Archives Collection]*

**183. TRENCH HALT, 1963**
Another of the minimal facility halts opened by the GWR in the hope of boosting traffic was this one at Trench.
*[M. E. M. Lloyd / WRRC]*

**184. ELLESMERE, 1962**
GWR Collett '14xx' Class 0-4-2T 1438 waits at Ellesmere with a train for Wrexham formed
of a single Autocoach on 26 May 1962.  *[M. A. King]*

**185. ELLESMERE, c.1950**

A view of Ellesmere station, looking towards Whitchurch, showing the impressive station buildings and ornate canopy. The station name board lists all the main stations on the line to Wrexham. A '2251' Class 0-6-0 shunts the yard while a Pannier Tank may be seen under the footbridge with the inevitable Autocoach. *[Lens of Sutton]*

**186. ELLESMERE, 1962**

GWR Collett '2251' Class 0-6-0 2204 awaits the ground signal allowing exit from the yard. The full height signal box seen in this view is a 'second generation' design supplied by Duttons between 1892 and 1895. Interesting details include arched windows to the locking room, decorative bargeboards and finials and a canopy to the porch; all indicative of the splendid attention to detail made by the railway builders. Note the token pick up posts with their oil lamps, for night illumination, on either side of the main line. [R. W. Thomson]

# The Oswestry–Gobowen Branch

Oswestry first appeared in the title of a proposed railway in June 1845 when Parliament authorised the Act for the Shrewsbury, Oswestry & Chester Junction Railway, which in fact bypassed the town! The proposal was promoted by the directors of the North Wales Mineral Railway whose own line from Wrexham to Chester was authorised in August 1844 and supplemented by a southerly extension to Ruabon authorised in July 1845. The need to serve Oswestry was addressed by a further Act in July 1846 which proposed a branch from Gobowen to Crickheath, south of the town. In fact the line was only built as far as Oswestry and this $2^1/_2$ mile branch opened in December 1848.

After several years of intense railway politics the Shrewsbury & Chester Railway, formed by the amalgamation of the SOCJ and the NWMR by an Act of July 1846, amalgamated with the Great Western Railway in September 1854. At this time the Great Western was still the only railway serving Oswestry, the Oswestry to Pool Quay section of what was to become the Cambrian Railways did not open until May 1860 while the Oswestry, Ellesmere and Whitchurch followed four years later.

Even after the Cambrian Railways became fully established with its headquarters at Oswestry the GWR retained a separate station, opening a replacement for their original terminus in 1866. Following the Cambrian's amalgamation with the Great Western in 1922 some major modernisation work took place in the Oswestry area. As far as the Gobowen branch was concerned the most important of these was the provision of a north-facing bay platform at the former Cambrian station which allowed the 1866 GWR station to be closed in July 1924 and converted into a goods station, in which role it survived until December 1971.

Passenger services on the Gobowen branch were withdrawn in November 1966, almost two years after the Whitchurch and Welshpool services. There was one intermediate station on the branch, Park Hall Halt, which was opened in 1926 to serve the nearby hospital and remained in use until the withdrawal of passenger services.

Disused and overgrown, the branch remains in place today and reopening with some form of local authority backing remains a possibility.

**187. GOBOWEN, 1956**

GWR 0-6-0PT 5416 stands in the bay platform at Gobowen at the head of an Oswestry train.

*[H. B. Priestley - Pacer Archives Collection]*

**188. GOBOWEN, 1962**

In the final years of steam traction on the Gobowen-Oswestry service the influence of the London Midland Region of British Rail is evident as LMS 'Ivatt' Class 2 2-6-2T 41285 departs with the auto-train working.

*[D. Johnson]*

**189. GOBOWEN, 1969**

A view towards Shrewsbury showing Gobowen South signal box, which controlled the Oswestry branch junction visible to the left of the warning notice. *[H. B. Priestley - Pacer Archives Collection]*

**190. PARK HALL, 1962**

The only intermediate stop between Gobowen and Oswestry was at Park Hall, which conveniently served the Orthopaedic Hospital. The auto-train calls to collect passengers who have probably been hospital visitors. *[M. A. King]*

**191. PARK HALL,** *c*.1965

In the final years of the Gobowen - Oswestry service two car DMUs were used, as typified by this Derby built set leaving Park Hall for Oswestry. The signal is the fixed distant for Gobowen South. *[M. Mensing]*

**192. PARK HALL, 1976**

Following closure of the railways to Oswestry they soon became the focus of preservationists. In support of their cause a special train ran in May 1976 which boasted very unusual motive power in the form of a Chester-based diesel parcels unit, which were affectionately referred to by railwaymen as 'Sputniks'. *[A. Bodlander]*

**193. OSWESTRY, 1926**

GWR 'Duke' 4-4-0 *Tregenna* stands outside the shed on a sunny August day while its crew pose for the photographer. Of note is the fire devil provided to keep the water column from freezing in cold weather. *[H. C. Casserley]*

# Oswestry Station, Shed & Works

### Introduction

Although little evidence remains today, for a century between the 1860s and 1960s Oswestry was an important secondary railway centre. Like many other railway centres, Oswestry's standing in Britain's railway network was brought about more by the rivalry between various competing companies attempting to control potential traffic flows, in this case between England and Mid Wales, than by consideration for the transport needs of the people and businesses of Oswestry.

The decision of the Cambrian Railways, formed in 1864 by the amalgamation of the Oswestry & Newtown, Oswestry, Ellesmere & Whitchurch, Llanidloes & Newtown and Newtown & Machynlleth Railways, to establish their headquarters at Oswestry made it a railway town for the next one hundred years. The growth of the town's population, from 5,414 in 1861 to 7,306 in 1871 and 9,479 in 1901 was undoubtedly due at least in part to the coming of the railways.

### The Station

Oswestry's first station opened in December 1848 as the terminus of the Shrewsbury & Chester Railway's branch from Gobowen. This remained the railhead for Mid Wales until the Oswestry & Newtown Railway opened in 1861, its station in Oswestry being alongside but separate from that of the S&C which had become part of the GWR in 1854.

With the complete opening of the Oswestry, Ellesmere & Whitchurch Railway in July 1864 and the formation of the Cambrian Railways the same year the O&N station gained importance. 1866 saw the opening of the impressive Italianate style building housing both station and headquarters office facilities which remains to this day.

Following the amalgamation of the Cambrian Railways with the GWR in 1922 the GWR carried out various improvements to the Cambrian station including the addition of a new bay platform for Gobowen trains, the extension of the down platform and the removal of a ticket platform which had previously stood outside the station. As a result of the improvements Gobowen trains began using the Cambrian station from July 1924 although the GWR station was retained for goods use.

Through passenger trains on the former Cambrian main line ceased in January 1965 with those to Gobowen following in November 1966.

**194. OSWESTRY, 1999**
This distinctive building combined station and headquarters of the Cambrian Railways in its heyday. It is built in an Italianate style of architecture and has recently been restored.  *[Authors' Collection]*

## The Shed

The Oswestry & Newtown Railway opened a locomotive shed in the town in 1861, a facility which was to remain part of the town's railway scene through Cambrian, GWR and BR days until eventual closure in 1965.

The shed was the largest on the Cambrian system and was located north of the station in the fork between the Gobowen and Whitchurch lines. In parallel with their improvements to the station following amalgamation, the GWR also modernised the motive power depot facilities by installing electric lighting, additional inspection pits, improved roof ventilation and a standard GWR design coaling stage.

In 1947 the six road shed had an allocation of 36 locomotives, mostly of GWR origin but including three ex-Cambrian 2-4-0Ts retained for working the Tanat Valley line. Even in 1961 there was still an allocation of some 30 locomotives of which over 20 were required to be in service to fulfil the daily workings for which the shed and its 100 enginemen were responsible.

## The Works

The first initiative to build a works at Oswestry was taken in April 1863 when the Oswestry & Newtown Railway asked Benjamin Piercy, a prominent railway engineer of the day, to prepare plans for a repair shop and carriage works. By August of that year the O&N had agreed in principle to the works being built at a cost of £28,000. However, nothing happened.

By the time the Cambrian Railways came into being in July 1864 the need for a repair works was becoming urgent. At the Company's first board meeting Thomas Savin, the contractor responsible for the construction of the new Company's constituent railways, was asked to prepare specifications. The design was carried out by Manchester locomotive builders Sharp, Stewart & Company. At this time Savin had a small workshop at Welshpool and this prompted the citizens of that town to urge the Cambrian board to locate their facility there in preference to Oswestry. The board were unmoved, however, and went ahead with the Oswestry scheme. Savin was awarded the contract to build the works which was equipped with Sharp, Stewart machinery. The works was in partial use by January 1866 when Savin's business empire failed and the Cambrian were obliged to complete the construction themselves. When the works opened fully in August 1866 the Welshpool shops closed.

Oswestry Works were built north east of the station in a part of the town known as the Shelf. The works were laid out from west to east as follows:

At the west end were a gas oil works and the erecting shops.
In the centre were offices, wash houses and the stores.
At the east end were the carriage and wagon works and the paint shop.

The erecting shop had a central traverser serving twelve roads on each side including the entrance and the through road which were always kept clear. Other roads could accommodate a single locomotive and tender. Locomotives were moved by the tedious method of 'pinching' as far as the yard outside the shop where the works shunter took over. At the other end of the works a network of sidings fanned out across a yard and eleven roads, including the through road, entered the carriage and wagon shops. A two foot gauge tramway ran the length of the carriage & wagon works and out to a timber drying store.

Many new carriages and wagons were built at Oswestry but only two locomotives were ever built there, although many extensive rebuilds were also carried out. Oswestry locomotive works saw a full century of service before finally being closed by British Railways on 31 December 1966, being the last GWR works to overhaul steam locomotives. The carriage & wagon works had closed two years previously during 1964.

**195. OSWESTRY, 1949**
An unusual visiting locomotive on the Gobowen auto-train is an ex-LNER (formerly GCR) C13 4-4-2T, possibly running in after repair at Oswestry or having arrived from Wrexham via Ellesmere. These locomotives were normally based at Wrexham Rhosddu shed for working services to Seacombe and Chester by the former GCR route.
*[R. S. Carpenter – Millbrook House Collection]*

**196. OSWESTRY, 1957**
GWR Collett 0-6-0 2255 stands at Oswestry Station with a train for Welshpool. The impressive buildings, which dominated the station, can be clearly seen.
*[N. C. Simmons]*

**197. OSWESTRY, c.1962**

An unidentified GWR 2-6-0 with a short train from Whitchurch awaits departure. To the right can be seen the former GWR passenger terminus for trains to Gobowen. Following amalgamation of the Great Western and Cambrian railways this became a goods depot.   *[E. N. Kneale]*

**198. OSWESTRY, 1964**

The decline in traffic is now becoming noticeable with far fewer wagons in evidence at the goods station. A GWR 0-6-0PT is shunting a few vans while the main line signal has been cleared for a train to Whitchurch. In the Gobowen bay the new order in the form of a 2 car DMU may be seen.

*[Mike Lloyd]*

**199. OSWESTRY, 1926**

A classic scene with GWR 4-4-0 1082, built at Oswestry in 1901 as Cambrian 19, passing under the north end signal gantry while a tank engine shunts freight wagons in the yard. The footbridge to the works is a prominent feature of this location.   *[H. C. Casserley]*

**200. OSWESTRY, 1935**

A view towards the North signal box and the engine shed with a '517' Class 0-4-2T on the auto-train from Gobowen. These small locomotives were ultimately replaced by the Collett '14xx' class. *[R. S. Carpenter – H. F. Wheeler collection]*

**201. OSWESTRY, *c*.1900**

In this view it is not readily apparent that the two roads on the right are a later addition as the decorative brickwork extends across all six roads. However, close inspection reveals various differences including the smoke vents in the roof, the use of lead flashing instead of ridge tiles and a steel joist across the doorway instead of arched brickwork. The two locomotives standing outside the shed are Cambrian 4-4-0s 70 and 71 built in 1894 by Sharp, Stewart & Co. *[M. E. M. Lloyd Collection]*

**202. OSWESTRY, 1935**

'Imported' from south Wales as a result of the Great Western takeover is this former Alexandra Docks Railway 0-6-0ST 680.
*[R. S. Carpenter – H. F. Wheeler Collection]*

**203. OSWESTRY, 1926**

GWR 4-4-0 1031, a former Sharp Stewart built Cambrian locomotive, after it had been 'Great Westernised' with modifications to the safety valve and chimney. *[H. C. Casserley]*

**204. OSWESTRY, 1935**

Another selection of modified former Cambrian locomotives are 0-6-0s 844 & 896. Also in this view is 2-4-0T 1197 which, together with 1196, usually worked the Tanat Valley line.  [*R. S. Carpenter – H. F. Wheeler collection*]

**205. OSWESTRY SHED, *c*.1960**
A superb shot of GWR 'Manor' Class 4-6-0 7819 *Hinton Manor* with every detail picked out in the light from the shed entrance. The smoke troughs can be clearly seen in the roof space.   [*E. N. Kneale*]

**206. OSWESTRY SHED, *c*.1963**
GWR 'County' Class 4-6-0 1002 *County of Berks* stands at the back of the shed with its motion stripped down for repair. [*E. N. Kneale*]

*Facing Top:*
**207. OSWESTRY WORKS, *c*.1960**
Most of the works buildings are visible in this view which also shows a GWR 0-6-0PT on pilot duties.  [*Brian Taylor*]

*Facing bottom:* **208. OSWESTRY WORKS, 1963**
The former Glasgow & South Western Railway 0-6-0T from Hafod Colliery seen during its repose after withdrawal and before its return to Glasgow for preservation. Perhaps with some irony the shed staff have painted LMS on the side tank.
[*E. N. Kneale*]

**209. OSWESTRY WORKS, 1963**

This view of the forge in the carriage & wagon works is full of interesting detail. The craftsman is leaning against a hydraulic press and around the walls are a number of hearths. Lengths of chain, buffers and other sundry items are stacked by the hearths while behind the ladder to the left are a quantity of wagon draw hooks. The item prominent in the foreground is an inverted wagon 'W-iron'.  *[E. N. Kneale]*

**210. OSWESTRY WORKS, 1963**

A visitor from Shrewsbury was LMS 'Jubilee' Class 4-6-0 45572 *Eire* which was receiving attention to its motion. *[E. N. Kneale]*

**211. OSWESTRY WORKS, 1963**

One of the works' craftsmen crouched inside the smokebox of GWR 0-6-2T 6625.

*[E. N. Kneale]*

**212. OSWESTRY WORKS, 1963**

It was usual practice for locomotives to be separated from their tenders when in works for attention. This separation provides a clear view of the footplate of LMS 'Jubilee' Class 4-6-0 45572 *Eire* which, from the quantity of firebricks stacked on the footplate, appears to be receiving attention to the brick arch in its firebox.

*[E. N. Kneale]*

**213. OSWESTRY, 1970**

By the time this photograph was taken Oswestry South signal box was only handling goods traffic, through passenger trains having ceased in 1965. The sidings behind the box were still receiving coal wagons for the local merchant. The broken windows suggest that the box was only open for a few hours each day and subject to vandalism when closed.

*[Mike Lloyd/WRRC]*

**214. OSWESTRY, 1999**
Happily the structure of the Oswestry South signal box still exists and is in the custody of the Cambrian Railways Society whose aim is to restore rail services to Oswestry.  *[Dave Southern]*

# The Cambrian
# Main Line –
# Whitchurch to
# Welshpool

The railway between Whitchurch and Welshpool was built during the 1860s by two different railway companies, both of which were based on Oswestry and were to become constituents of the Cambrian Railways.

The Oswestry, Ellesmere & Whitchurch Railway Act received the royal assent on 1 August 1861 with construction work starting soon afterwards. The 10³/₄ miles from Whitchurch to Ellesmere passed over a three mile stretch of Whixall Moss which presented a major obstacle to construction. The technique of laying bales of brushwood on the moss and building the track bed above was adopted. Single track was laid on a double line formation and intermediate stations were provided at Welshampton, Bettisfield and Fenn's Bank. The line opened to goods in April 1863 and to passengers the following month.

The section between Ellesmere and Oswestry, construction of which also required peat bogs to be crossed, was provided with an intermediate station at Whittington where the line crossed the Shrewsbury & Chester Railway. The line opened in July 1864, permitting through services to begin between Whitchurch and Oswestry. A station was opened at Frankton in 1866 and a halt was opened at Tinkers Green, between Oswestry and Whittington, in October 1939 to serve the adjacent military facilities.

Ellesmere, the most important intermediate station between Whitchurch and Oswestry, became a junction in November 1895 when the branch to Wrexham via Bangor-on-Dee and Marchwiel, as described elsewhere in this book, was opened.

The railway between Oswestry and Welshpool was part of the Oswestry & Newtown Railway, the Act for which received the royal assent in June 1855. Construction began at Llanymynech working towards Oswestry. The section between Oswestry and Pool Quay, built as a single track on double line formation, was opened in May 1860. The remainder of the line on to Welshpool, including two crossings of the River Severn, opened in August of the same year. Intermediate stations were provided on opening at Llynclys, Llanymynech, Four Crosses and Pool Quay with Ardleen and Pant added in 1864. The station at Buttington Junction, where the line from Shrewsbury met the Oswestry & Newtown for the parallel run into Welshpool, was opened at the same time as the LNWR (later to become LNWR & GWR joint) line in January 1862. Later improvements

**215. WHITCHURCH, c.1960**

A view of Whitchurch station looking south towards Shrewsbury. The Cambrian line can just be seen diverging to the right beyond Cambrian Junction signal box. On the platform may be seen a number of racing pigeon baskets awaiting dispatch. The locomotive shed was situated off to the left of the photograph.

*[Lens of Sutton]*

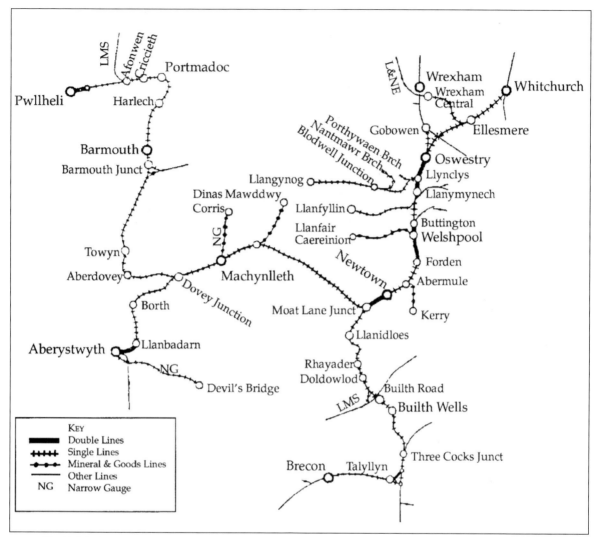

*The GWR's Oswestry District stretched far beyond the town's boundaries to Pwllheli, Aberystwyth and Brecon. This map, redrawn from the cover of the March 1943 Sectional Appendix, identifies double and single line sections, mineral lines, narrow gauge lines and junctions with lines of other districts.*

included the conversion of the two single lines between Buttington Junction and Welshpool to double track and doubling between Oswestry and Llanymynech.

Both the Oswestry, Ellesmere & Whitchurch and the Oswestry & Newtown became part of the Cambrian Railways on its formation in July 1864. Oswestry became the headquarters of the Cambrian and an important railway centre. In 1922 the Cambrian amalgamated with the Great Western and although the GWR made various improvements the pre-grouping character remained until the early years of the British Railways era. The decision of Beeching's 'Reshaping of British Railways' report to concentrate all traffic to and from the Cambrian Coast via Shrewsbury meant that Whitchurch to Welshpool closed to through traffic during January 1965. Freight to Ellesmere continued for two more months while the section from Oswestry to Llynclys remains intact to this day as the middle section of what is now a mothballed freight-only branch from Gobowen to Blodwell Quarry. South of Llynclys the Cambrian Railways Trust has relaid track towards Pant and began a heritage train service in the summer of 2007, with ambitions to ultimately link Gobowen and Welshpool via Oswestry by rail once again.

**216. WHITCHURCH, *c*.1965**
The diesel age at Whitchurch as an unidentified Class 47 arrives on a passenger working. Track tamping machines are stabled in the former Chester line bay platform. *[E. N. Kneale]*

**217. WHITCHURCH, 1959**

A fine view of the informative name board at the north end of Whitchurch station. GWR 'Manor' Class 4-6-0 7803 *Barcote Manor* has just arrived with a train from the Cambrian lines. Note in the distance the suspension bridge which carries a footpath over the sidings and running lines.

*[H. B. Priestley - Pacer Archives Collection]*

**218. WHITCHURCH, *c*.1970**

A view from the footbridge looking towards Shrewsbury. The lifted route of the former Cambrian line is still clearly visible beyond the signal box which can just be seen behind the water tank. Note the removal of the signal arm for the branch and the modernity provided by fluorescent lighting.  *[E. N. Kneale]*

**219. FENN'S BANK, 1959**

Fenn's Bank was the first passing place on the single line from Whitchurch. There was a small goods yard, seen on the right of this view, which dealt primarily with domestic coal and agricultural traffic. At the south end of the station there was a private siding serving the aluminium refinery of H. H. Wardle (Metals) Ltd. *[H. B. Priestley - Pacer Archives Collection]*

**220. BETTISFIELD, 1959**

The signalman exchanges tokens with the driver of an Oswestry bound freight despite there being apparatus for the purpose at the bottom of the signal box steps. As at Fenn's Bank there was a loop for passing trains and sidings but only one platform. *[H. B. Priestley - Pacer Archives Collection]*

**221. BETTISFIELD, *c*.1960**

A close up of the station building and its raised letter name board. The advertising posters encourage travel to Prestatyn and the Isle of Man. *[Lens of Sutton]*

**222. BETTISFIELD, 1962**

A limited stop service from Whitchurch to Welshpool hauled by GWR 2-6-0 6378 stands in the platform-less loop at Bettisfield while GWR 'Manor' Class 4-6-0 7803 *Barcote Manor* runs in past the signal box and token exchange apparatus with a local train for Whitchurch. *[M. A. King]*

**223. WELSHAMPTON, *c*.1910**

The local coal merchant is about to load his cart with Staffordshire coal from two wagons standing on the single siding provided at Welshampton. Some of the station buildings may be seen behind the wagons while the station house is just visible to the extreme right. *[Lens of Sutton]*

**224. WELSHAMPTON, *c*.1960**

The station porter steps out to meet a Whitchurch bound stopping train hauled by GWR 2-6-0 6335. There do not appear to be any waiting passengers, but presumably he has to load the small milk churn.  *[H. B. Priestley - Pacer Archives Collection]*

**225. ELLESMERE, 1956**

A Whitchurch–Oswestry stopping train hauled by GWR 'Dukedog' Class 4-4-0 9021 arriving at Ellesmere.  *[Lens of Sutton]*

**226. FRANKTON, *c*.1910**

A view of the rather grand station house at Frankton. On the end wall nearest the photographer may be seen the embossed brick Cambrian Railways crest. The station house is believed to have been the residence of a senior Cambrian Railways official. *[Lens of Sutton]*

**227. FRANKTON, 1962**

A close up of the Cambrian Railways crest in the pediment of the gable wall. Of interest, especially as it is on one of their own buildings, is that the wording refers to the Cambrian Railway rather than Cambrian Railways. *[Authors' Collection]*

**228. FRANKTON, 1962**

By the time this photograph was taken Frankton station had been demoted to the status of a Halt. LMS Ivatt Class 2 2-6-0 46507 arrives with a two coach local working. *[H. B. Priestley - Pacer Archives Collection]*

**229. WHITTINGTON, *c*.1959**

The Cambrian station at Whittington was known as 'High Level' to distinguish it from the 'Low Level' station below it on the Shrewsbury–Chester line. The Cambrian station closed in January 1960, five years before the line itself. In this view the signal box on the platform provided to control the passing loop can be clearly seen. Goods traffic was not handled but a solitary wagon can be seen in the short siding beyond the platform. *[Lens of Sutton]*

**230. LLYNCLYS, 1961**

A view showing the main station building. The small timber shelter on the opposite platform replaced a more substantial former Cambrian structure. Beyond the over bridge can be seen one of the abutments of the Crickheath Tramway bridge and beyond that is a hut housing a ground frame which controlled access to a siding known as 'Haystack Siding'. *[Stations UK]*

**231. LLYNCLYS, 1958**

In this earlier view of GWR 2-6-0 6335 arriving with a Welshpool bound train the original building is still intact. In the background can be seen Llynclys Junction where the Tanat Valley line diverged.  *[H. B. Priestley - Pacer Archives Collection]*

**232. LLYNCLYS, 2006**

Llynclys is the base of another preservation group, the Cambrian Railways Trust. The relationship with the neighbouring Cambrian Railways Society at Oswestry and Nantmawr has been tempestuous in the past but both now agree that they have roles to play in the restoration of former Cambrian lines in the area.  *[A. Bodlander]*

**233. LLYNCLYS, 2006**

A neatly restored Metro-Cammell DMU belonging to the Cambrian Railways Trust. This group ran their first steam hauled public train at Llynclys on 24 August 2007.  *[A. Bodlander]*

**234. PANT, 1963**

A view of the signal box and platforms at Pant station. A goods siding was also provided. Treadle worked bells were provided to warn the porter/signalman on duty of approaching trains. *[H. B. Priestley - Pacer Archives Collection]*

**235. PANT, *c*.1920**

A view looking across the Shropshire Union Canal towards Pant station where the level crossing gates and signal box may be clearly seen. Below the signal box can be seen the small arch through which passed the narrow gauge tramway from the quarries at Crickheath Hill. The narrow boat is probably awaiting a cargo of local stone. *[John Ryan Collection]*

**236. LLANYMYNECH, *c*.1912**

An early twentieth century view of the two stations at Llanymynech. The primitive one on the extreme left served the erstwhile Potteries, Shrewsbury and North Wales Railway which closed twice during its short life before rising again as the Shropshire and Montgomeryshire Railway in 1911 under the management of Colonel H.F. Stephens, a famed promoter of light railways. *[Authors' Collection]*

**237. LLANYMYNECH, 1932**

A former Cambrian 0-6-0, by now GWR 849, passes on a southbound train. The Shropshire and Montgomeryshire Railway sidings can be seen behind the name board, which advises travellers to change here for the Llanfyllin branch. *[H. C. Casserley]*

**238. LLANYMYNECH, 1935**

A delightful period picture of the Llanfyllin branch train after arrival at Llanymynech. The pristine GWR 'B' set coaches are in stark contrast to the older vehicles consigned to the siding. The locomotive is GWR 58xx Class 0-4-2T 5816. The 14xx class was a variant of this type fitted for auto-train working. *[R. S. Carpenter – H. F. Wheeler collection]*

**239. LLANYMYNECH, 1948**

A view from the footbridge looking towards Welshpool. The lines of the former Shropshire & Montgomeryshire Railway run in on the left with the Llanfyllin branch junction forking right beyond the signal box.
*[R. S. Carpenter – P. J. Garland Collection]*

**240. FOUR CROSSES, 1963**

This view of Four Crosses shows the staggered platforms and the GWR signal box situated adjacent to the barrow crossing between the two platforms. The goods yard was situated off to the left of the picture. An interesting special instruction applicable to Four Crosses was that because the platform under the road bridge was only three feet wide, the Station Master was responsible for placing a member of staff there when long trains called in order to 'caution passengers against passing along'. *[H. B. Priestley - Pacer Archives Collection]*

**241. FOUR CROSSES, c.1910**

Four Crosses station with a freight train passing. The wagons include two from Black Park Colliery at Chirk and a roofed lime wagon. The goods yard crane and associated buildings can be seen to the left of the station building, which is similar in design to the one at Welshampton. *[Lens of Sutton]*

**242. POOL QUAY, *c*.1963**
A short local train arrives hauled by a BR Standard Class 4 2-6-4T 80079. This locomotive is now preserved on the Severn Valley Railway. *[Authors' Collection]*

**243. BUTTINGTON, *c*.1955**
GWR 'Dukedog' Class 4-4-0 9001 heads through Buttington with a special working, possibly a troop train, formed of former Southern Railway stock. Ornamental bargeboards are a prominent architectural feature of the station buildings. *[R. K. Blencowe]*

**244. BUTTINGTON,** *c.1930*

A train for Shrewsbury leaves Buttington. The way in which the Shrewsbury and Oswestry lines became single immediately beyond the station is apparent in this view. *[Stations UK]*

**245.WELSHPOOL, 1958**

An overall view at Welshpool, looking east, in steam days. GWR 2-6-0 6378 is moving through the station 'light engine' whilst GWR 'Manor' Class 4-6-0 7803 *Barcote Manor* is standing at the island platform with a train of four corridor coaches.
*[H. B. Priestley - Pacer Archives Collection]*

**246. WELSHPOOL, 1958**

7803 *Barcote Manor* has run forward from its train. Empty wagons can be seen in the sidings.
*[H. B. Priestley - Pacer Archives Collection]*

**247. WELSHPOOL, 2005**
The realigned railway at Welshpool which maintains its passing facility and is provided with an engineers' siding. The passenger facilities are reduced to a basic 'bus shelter' pattern. *[A. Bodlander]*

**248. WELSHPOOL, 2005**

A view showing the bypass road following the former railway route. The former station building now houses craft and tourist shops.    *[A. Bodlander]*

**249. WELSHPOOL, *c*.1950**
In its railway heyday Welshpool was linked to Llanfair Caereinion by a narrow gauge line providing interchange facilities for both goods and passengers. The passenger service succumbed to road competition in 1931 but the freight service survived until 1956. A typical freight train is seen here with the main line station in the background.
*[Hugh Davies]*

**250. WELSHPOOL, *c*.1956**
Prior to its final demise the narrow gauge railway became popular with enthusiasts anxious to travel the line. A typical party is assembling here at Welshpool. It is fortunate that many who travelled were inspired to start a movement to preserve the line. *[Hugh Davies – AB Collection]*

# The Llanfyllin Branch

The town of Llanfyllin can claim to be an early adopter of integrated public transport, as in August 1860 the landlord of the Red Lion Inn, Mr Edward Lloyd, began an omnibus service from the town to connect with certain morning and evening trains at Llanymynech on the Oswestry & Newtown Railway.

In September of that year the promoters of the West Midland, Shrewsbury and Coast of Wales Railway proposed to put Llanfyllin on the railway map as part of their grand scheme to link the Severn Valley and Shrewsbury & Welshpool Railways via Llanymynech, 'near Llanfyllin', Llangynog and thence by tunnel through the Berwyns to Llandrillo, from where there would be a branch to Corwen. However, the down-to-earth citizens of Llanfyllin favoured a simple branch to the Oswestry & Newtown at Llanymynech and at a public meeting in the town in October 1860 a committee was formed and early pledges of funding were secured from Lord Powis and the local MP, Mr D Pugh. Other local committees were formed in several of the settlements along the proposed route of the branch.

The sod-cutting ceremony took place at Llanfyllin in September 1861 and included all those features which by then were becoming traditional – a triumphal arch, a grand procession with bands and regalia, a silver spade, a banquet for the great and the good, treats for local children and a firework display to round off the day. The sod was cut by Mrs Dugdale, wife of the High Sheriff of Montgomeryshire, who was presented with a silver spade and barrow by the contractor, Thomas Savin. The Act authorising construction had received the Royal Assent in May 1861 but Benjamin Piercy's survey had been delayed until 'after the harvest to avoid damage to crops'. By December, however, the navvies were at work and early in 1862 the local press were announcing that a carriage would operate on the line from Llanymynech as far as Llansantffraid to connect with the omnibus from Llanfyllin, which would then be able to make an additional round trip.

The line was sufficiently complete by March 1863 to enable *Nant Clwyd*, a Manning Wardle 0-6-0ST locomotive owned by Savin and previously used on the construction of the Denbigh, Ruthin & Corwen Railway, to reach Llanfyllin and cause a large turnout of onlookers. The first passenger train ran the following month when Mr & Mrs Dugdale, family and entourage arrived at Llanfyllin after a nine hour journey by  through carriage from Brighton which must rank as one of the more unusual workings onto the branch. What could be claimed to be the first public train ran one evening in early June to convey participants to a concert in Llanfyllin in aid of Bwlch-y-cibau church, although this preceded the official inspection and approval of the Board of Trade. The official opening took place in July 1863, the day being marked by a special excursion to the Cardigan Bay resort of Borth, 'Fares 5s and 2s 6d, including return', which is likely to have provided some of Llanfyllin's inhabitants with their first view of the sea. Following the return of the excursion a dinner presided over by Mr Dugdale took place in a pavilion adjoining the station. A service of five trains per day was offered between Oswestry and Llanfyllin with the fare initially being set at 1s 9d Third Class return.

Traffic was boosted in 1881 when work commenced on the Lake Vyrnwy reservoir for Liverpool Corporation. A special train ran from Birkenhead Woodside conveying dignitaries from Liverpool and collected local worthies at Oswestry before proceeding to Llanfyllin from where a convoy of thirty horse-drawn vehicles took them to the foundation stone ceremony. Throughout construction Llanfyllin was the railhead for the delivery of materials to the site and a stable of 95 heavy horses was maintained for the task. Following completion of the reservoir it became a popular destination for excursions which provided an important source of traffic for the line. The Cambrian's amalgamation with the Great Western Railway in 1921 and nationalisation in 1948 had little effect on the operation of the branch but ultimately Dr Beeching's 'Reshaping of British Railways' report decreed that it should close. Closure came in January 1965 at the same time as the Whitchurch to Welshpool section of the Cambrian main line and the Ruabon to Barmouth line, with track lifting taking place the following year.

**251. LLANSANTFFRAID, *c*.1900**

This early view of the station shows the spelling which prevailed until 1922. The structure is quite substantial with a two-storey Stationmaster's house and a single storey wing providing the station accommodation. The architecture is typical Cambrian cottage style with decorative bargeboards to the roof. *[Lens of Sutton]*

**252. LLANSANTFFRAID, *c*.1960**

A Llanfyllin bound train arriving hauled by an LMS Ivatt Class 2 2-6-0 running tender-first. The signalman and driver are about to change the token for the single line from Llanymynech for a tablet which was applicable for the rest of the journey to Llanfyllin. In the left foreground the point blades to the passing loop can just be seen. There was access to sidings and a warehouse, used primarily for agricultural traffic, from the loop. *[Authors' Collection]*

### 253. LLANSANTFFRAID, *c.*1955

Another view of a token / tablet exchange at Llansantffraid with a three coach train hauled by GWR Collett 0-4-2T 5806. The line was originally controlled by the tablet system throughout, but the electric token was introduced for the lower section after the GWR made alterations at Llanymynech. The rural idyll of the branch railway station is well demonstrated by the flowerbeds and general tidiness. *[Authors' Collection]*

### 254. LLANFECHAIN, *c.*1960

An unidentified LMS Ivatt Class 2 2-6-0 locomotive and two coach train arrives at Llanfechain from Oswestry. Note the coal merchant's lorry and a fine Leyland HGV in the station yard. It is on record that there was once a signal box situated behind the station nameboard, but it is uncertain if it was ever a block post. *[H. B. Priestley - Pacer Archives Collection]*

**255. BRYNGWYN, *c.*1890**

Bryngwyn – in the early days of the railway known as Brongwyn – was described as a station in this early view. However, it displays the characteristics of a request stop with a signal for operation by intending passengers wishing to stop a train. *[John Ryan Collection]*

**256. BRYNGWYN, *c.*1960**

A later view after the fixed signals had given way to hand signals consistent with re-designation as a halt. Despite this it is recorded that on busy market days a booking clerk was dispatched from Llanfyllin to issue tickets.  *[Lens of Sutton]*

**257. LLANFYLLIN, 1932**
An evocative view from the 1930s. The four-wheel coaches appear to have received their GWR chocolate and cream livery.
The 'period' passengers are also worthy of closer scrutiny. *[H. C. Casserley]*

**258. LLANFYLLIN, 1956**
A view from the buffer stops showing the extent of the passenger and goods facilities. *[R. K. Blencowe]*

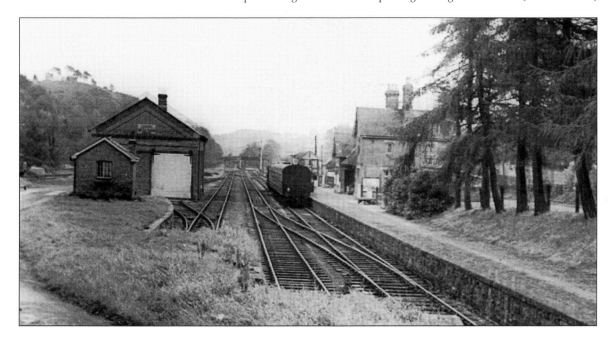

**259. LLANFYLLIN, 1962**

A busy time with LMS Ivatt Class 2 2-6-0 46511 preparing an Oswestry bound freight whilst sister engine 46512 is at the head of the passenger train for Oswestry. Note the site of the former cattle dock in front of the signal box where the mineral wagon in berthed. Behind the camera is the site of the engine shed.   [*David Wilson*]

# Railways in the
# Tanat Valley

A route through the Tanat Valley had been proposed in the prospectus for the West Midlands, Shrewsbury and Coast of Wales Railway in 1860. There had been a variety of earlier schemes for routes through Mid and North Wales but their objective had been to secure a route and a port for Irish traffic, rather than considering any local needs. Two locations, Porth Dinllaen and Holyhead, vied for the distinction of being the port for Ireland. Routes to both presented considerable engineering obstacles but Holyhead and the route from Chester along the North Wales coast and across Anglesey was ultimately favoured.

The subsequent development of railways in the Tanat Valley, however, is linked to more local issues, primarily the exploitation of minerals. This prompted the establishment of a railhead at Porthywaen in 1863 as the terminus of a short branch from the Oswestry & Newtown Railway, one of the constituents of the Cambrian Railways. There had been various tramroads established in the late eighteenth and early nineteenth centuries in the Llanymynech and Porthywaen areas as feeders for mineral traffic to the Montgomery and Ellesmere (later the Shropshire Union) canals, and the development of new rail links was a natural progression.

The next important development was the opening of the Nantmawr branch of the Potteries, Shrewsbury and North Wales Railway from Llanymynech. However, the 'Potts' was soon in financial difficulties and the owner of the Nantmawr quarries, a Mr France, was soon appealing to the Cambrian Railways to operate and maintain the line, which it agreed to do from 1881. In 1896 the Cambrian opened a new connection between the Nantmawr branch and the Llanfyllin branch, with the additional benefit of improving the working of the Llanfyllin branch at Llanymynech by removing an awkward uphill reversal movement at the start of the journey.

However, the physical and legal constraints of standard gauge railways were not an ideal response to the flexible needs of mining and quarrying, particularly in more isolated areas, but the passing of the Light Railways Act of 1896 made the expansion of industries further up the Tanat Valley a more attractive proposition. The Act empowered local authorities to support light railway schemes in their areas and had additional benefits in securing Treasury grants and loans while minimising opposition from local landowners. In 1897 the Cambrian's chief engineer, George Owen, provided his services to the promoters of the Tanat Valley Railway. His proposals were presented to the Light Railway Commissioners at Oswestry in August 1897 and a Light Railway Order was granted the following month, despite a rival bid from promoters of a narrow gauge line from Llanfyllin to Llangynog. Another challenge which had to be overcome was the insistence of a local landowner with interests in the Shropshire Railways Company, Viscount Newport, fourth Earl of Bradford, that the Tanat Valley line must cross the Nantmawr branch by means of a flyover. However, when the Cambrian took a lease on the Nantmawr branch from the Shropshire Railways Company in 1898 the Earl's influence on developments diminished.

The traditional sod-cutting ceremony with associated festivities was carried out at Porthywaen in September 1899 by the Countess of Powis. A mere ten days later cost estimates began to rise as the lowest tender received, that of Messrs Strachan of Cardiff, was approximately £1,000 higher than the estimates. Increased loans were secured from the Treasury and from Liverpool Corporation, whose interest had previously been attracted by the new railway's potential in assisting the construction of a pipeline from their new reservoir at Lake Vyrnwy to proposed filter beds at Llanforda near Oswestry. Construction of the line began in July 1901 but was beset by bad weather and difficulties with the contractor, who even began to operate his own unofficial passenger service between Llangynog and Porthywaen! Construction was ultimately completed and an opening ceremony was performed in January 1904 by the Dowager Lady Williams Wynn.

There were stations at Porthywaen, Blodwell Junction, Llanyblodwel, Llansilin Road, Llangedwyn, Pentrefelin, Llanrhaiadr Mochant, Pedairfford, Penybontfawr and Llangynog. Llangedwyn and Llanrhaiadr had two platforms with passing loops and open lever frames lever frames located on a simple plinth at the end of one of the platforms. The only signal boxes were at Blodwell Junction and Porthywaen, the latter being reduced in status to a ground frame in the 1930s. In true light railway fashion the stations had the simplest of buildings, with corrugated iron cladding on a timber frame. The final construction bill was in excess of £92,000, double the original estimates. A Receiver was appointed in April 1904 and the company remained in receivership until taken over by the Cambrian in March 1921.

Proposals for a 'west curve' at Llanyblodwel were made in order to enable through trains to operate between Llangynog and Llanfyllin but despite Viscount Newport arguing for construction of the chord a through coach exchanged at Llanyblodwel had to suffice and even this was withdrawn in 1917 due to lack of patronage. The possibility of the connection finally lapsed in 1921 and the remainder of the Llanymynech loop line, as the portion of the original Nantmawr branch between Llanyblodwel and the junction with the 1896 realignment of the Llanfyllin branch was known, fell into disuse in 1925 and had been lifted by 1938.

Distinctive motive power and occasional mixed trains characterised operations on the Tanat Valley line but the Second World War caused the passenger service to be reduced and a rival road service operated by Crosville Motor Services soon became established, leading to withdrawal of all passenger services in 1951 and freight beyond Llanrhaiadr Mochant the following year. In December 1960 flood damage to the piers of a river bridge west of Llangedwyn led to the line being cut back to Blodwell Junction. The remaining traffic was stone from Nantmawr and Blodwell quarries. Traffic from Nantmawr ceased in the early 1970s but that from Blodwell, principally ballast for British Rail, continued until October 1988. Remarkably the track of the Nantmawr branch remained in place following closure, although increasingly overgrown, and so provided the Oswestry-based Cambrian Railways Society with the location to develop as a heritage railway.

**260. LLYNCLYS, 1980**
For over a hundred years stone for ballast had been moved from the quarries in this area. Class 25 25110 propels wagons over the weighbridge as it makes up its train. *[Trefor Thompson]*

**261. LLYNCLYS, 1980**
With its train now complete 25110 departs for Gobowen in March 1980.  *[Trefor Thompson]*

**262. PORTHYWAEN, *c*.1935**
A view at Porthywaen taken about 1935. The locomotive is GWR 2-4-0T 1308 *Lady Margaret,* acquired by the GWR when it took over the Liskeard and Looe Railway in Cornwall in 1909. It was suited to light railway work and was transferred to Oswestry shortly after the Grouping in 1923. The train here is heading towards Llynclys from Whitehaven Quarry. The wagon repair works can just be seen behind the train. In the centre of the picture is the narrow gauge track of the Crickheath Tramway. *[Mike Lloyd Collection]*

**263. PORTHYWAEN, 1978**
With flagmen in attendance Class 25 25332 begins to cross the main road with a stone train from Llanddu Quarry.
*[Trefor Thompson]*

**264. PORTHYWAEN, 1978**
The flagman appears to be about to rejoin the train, obviously assuming that it is now prominent enough to be seen by any oncoming motorist. *[Trefor Thompson]*

**265. NANTMAWR, 1957**
A GWR 0-6-0PT in the run round loop adjacent to the Quarry branch which can be seen in the background.
*[C. H. A. Townley]*

**266. NANTMAWR, 2006**
A line-up of locomotives and equipment acquired by the Cambrian Railways Society preservation group now active on the branch. *[Dave Southern]*

**267. LLANGEDWYN, 1958**

Llangedwyn was originally a tablet station and passing place but the loop here was cut back to form a siding in 1922. The tablet section then became Blodwell Junction to Lanrhaiadr Mochnant. *[H. C. Casserley]*

**268. LLANRHAIADR MOCHNANT, 1944**

Mr W E Morris (Station Master) and son at the open ground frame which worked the station's points and signals. Did this early training for Morris junior result in succession to railway service, once a tradition in many families?

*[Authors' Collection]*

**269. LLANRHAIADR MOCHNANT, *c*.1910**
Using the concessions provided by the Light Railway Act of 1896 the Tanat Valley stations were of a simple corrugated iron construction. Obvious from this posed view is that the economies did not extend to staff in the early years. *[Lens of Sutton]*

**270. LLANRHAIADR MOCHNANT, *c*.1935**
2-4-0T 1196 arrives with a train of ancient six-wheeled stock bound for Oswestry. *[Authors' Collection]*

**271. LLANGYNOG, *c.*1952**

Llangynog originally had its own engine shed. To the right of this view can be seen the water tower and the inspection pit. In the right foreground the brick floor to the shed can just be discerned. *[Mike Lloyd / WRRC]*

**272. LLANGYNOG, *c.*1947**

GWR 2-4-0T 1196 at Llangynog prior to departure for Oswestry with a train formed of one bogie coach and two four-wheeled examples. *[IRS Ken Cooper Collection]*

# Llanforda Waterworks Railway

The water treatment works at Llanforda near Oswestry was built by Liverpool Corporation to filter water from Lake Vyrnwy destined for the city. The 2'0" railway at the works was used to assist in emptying and recharging the filter beds. The first locomotive recorded as being at the works was delivered in 1936 and the last left following closure of the railway in 1989. The following series of photographs were all taken in September 1985.

**273. LLANFORDA, 1985**
Sand is being loaded by hand into a skip wagon on temporary track laid on the floor of the drained filter bed.  *[Mark Hambly]*

**274. LLANFORDA, 1985**
As each skip was filled it was propelled to the end of the bed where it was lifted out by a road crane.  *[Mark Hambly]*

### 275. LLANFORDA, 1985
The locomotive in use for collecting the loaded train was a Ruston & Hornsby LBT Class four-wheel mechanical locomotive, works number 496039 built in February 1963. *[Mark Hambly]*

### 276. LLANFORDA, 1985
The completed train of four wagons is ready to make its way to the sand tip. *[Mark Hambly]*

### 277. LLANFORDA, 1985
On arrival at the sand tip the wagons are unloaded by being tipped manually. *[Mark Hambly]*

# Bibliography

Both Wrexham and Oswestry have featured in a number of other railway books but there has never been a book devoted specifically to the railways of and around the two towns. For the underpinning history of these railways and the wider context in which they were conceived, constructed, operated and closed there is probably nothing better than Peter Baughan's North & Mid Wales volume in the *Regional History of the Railways of Great Britain* series (David & Charles, 1980). The corresponding volume in the same publisher's *Forgotten Railways* series by Rex Christiansen (1976) provides historical facts, contemporary observation and atmosphere supported by a comprehensive gazetteer. The circumstances leading to the ultimately dominant role of the Great Western Railway in the area are discussed in *The Great Western North of Wolverhampton* by Keith Beck published by Ian Allan in 1986.

Vic Bradley's *Industrial Locomotives of North Wales* (Industrial Railway Society, 1992) is far more wide-ranging than the title suggests, containing a compact but detailed and comprehensively referenced history of every known location in the former counties of Clwyd and Gwynedd at which a railway system of 15" gauge or greater and worked by locomotives was used for industrial or pleasure purposes. For similar sites over the border in Shropshire the corresponding volume is *Industrial Locomotives of Cheshire, Shropshire and Herefordshire* by Alan Bridges (1977). The IRS also include contractors' operations associated with the building of main line railways within the scope of their Handbooks.

Both of the main 'home grown' companies in the area, the Cambrian and the WM&CQ, have been covered by respected railway historians. Rex Christiansen and R W Miller wrote a two part history of the *Cambrian Railways* (David & Charles, 1967 & 1968) in a format consistent with a number of other company histories to emerge from the Newton Abbott publishers in the 1960s and 1970s. R W Kidner's *The Cambrian Railways* (Oakwood Press) first appeared in 1954 with an enlarged second edition following in 1992, while the same publisher also produced histories of the *Tanat Valley Railway* by Wilfred Wren in 1979 and *Wrexham and Ellesmere Railway* by Stanley Jenkins and John Strange in 2004. James Boyd, probably better known for his studies of the narrow gauge lines further west, was responsible for a very comprehensive history of the *WM&CQ* (Oakwood Press, 1991) which also covered the Buckley Railway and associated pre-railway industrial tramroads in the Buckley and Queensferry areas.

Over the years the lines in the area have been covered to varying degrees in a number of photographic albums. Two in particular stand out for the variety of the pictures selected and the detail in the supporting text; C C Green's *North Wales Branch Line Album* (Ian Allan, 1983) and Rex Christiansen's *Chester & North Wales Border Railways* (Ian Allan, 2001).

In an age when much excellent material (and some of much more doubtful value) is available on the internet there are three websites which deserve a particular mention here.

- Dave Sallery's www.penmorfa.com has a wide range of north Wales railway and industrial heritage content, including a page devoted to the Wrexham to Bidston line.

- Dave Plimmer's www.2d53.co.uk is a collection of photographs, working timetables, trip notices, track plans and other miscellaneous content covering the railways of north and mid Wales during the 'blue diesel' era of the 1970s and early 1980s.

- Charlie Hulme's www.nwrail.org.uk is an on-line magazine devoted to the railways of north Wales, updated every few days with news reports, topical photographs and details of forthcoming happenings such as special train workings to and from the area, events on heritage railways and local railway society meetings.